STONKED!

How GameStop Stopped the Game and 5 Reasons Why it Should Matter to You

J.J. Wainwright

Minterleaf Holdings, LLC

Copyright © 2021 Minterleaf Holdings, LLC

All rights reserved

The characters and events portrayed in this book are fictitious. Any similarity to real persons, living or dead, is coincidental and not intended by the author.

No part of this book may be reproduced, or stored in a retrieval system, or transmitted in any form or by any means, electronic, mechanical, photocopying, recording, or otherwise, without express written permission of the publisher.

ISBN: 9798509627279
Independently Published

Cover design by: Art Painter
Library of Congress Control Number: 2018675309
Printed in the United States of America

CONTENTS

Chapter 1: Zooming in

Chapter 2: Stock Market Basics

Chapter 3: The Reddit Rebellion

Chapter 4: The Timeline of Events

Chapter 5: Irrational Exuberance or Something Else?

Chapter 6: Bi-Partisan Unity

Chapter 7: The Cryptocurrency Connection

Chapter 8: 5 Reasons It Should Matter to You

References

INTRODUCTION / CHAPTER 1

Zooming in

The GameStop Frenzy. The Reddit Rebellion. The French Revolution of Finance. Call it what you will. We are referring to the event, or rather the sequence of events, that transpired in the first months of 2021 sending the price of GameStop stock to exaggerated levels and forcing some Wall Street hedge funds to take billions of dollars in losses. It was the ultimate faceoff between Wall Street and Main Street; an unprecedented event that shook the world of high finance to its core. But why? How was it different from any other short squeeze that has happened in the past? We aim to answer that question in the following chapters of this book. Our thesis might surprise you so stick with us to the end.

Before we dive into the details, we need to baseline some stock market concepts and terminology. The following chapter is a review of the fundamental market concepts you need to have fresh in your mind to fully understand why the Reddit Rebellion was so controversial and historic—and of course, why it should matter to you at all.

If you already have a basic understanding of the stock market, what determines the price of a stock, and what options trading is, you could skip to the third section in Chapter 2 on short selling where we begin to discuss these basic concepts within the context of the GameStop story.

Let us begin.

CHAPTER 2

Stock Market Basics

Supply and Demand

What determines the price of a stock? The answer is simple. The price of a stock is determined by the same thing that determines the price of anything: supply and demand.

Each day that the stock market is open, stock prices move up and they move down depending on the number of buyers and sellers.

The level of *demand* is determined by the number of *buyers* who are willing to buy a stock at any given time at any given price.

The level of *supply* is determined by the number of *sellers* who are willing to sell a stock at any given time at any given price.

When corporate stock is purchased, buyers and sellers are exchanging money for fractional ownership. The most recent price at which a buyer has purchased a stock becomes that stock's new price that is publicly available to the market.

When demand levels increase, the company's share price tends to move higher (just like any other commodity or consumer product). When this happens, it often creates price momentum in a bullish (or positive) direction.

Conversely, when demand levels *decrease*, a company's share price tends to move lower often creating momentum in a bearish (or negative) direction.

Essentially, this correlation shows that the stock market works in much of the same way that any other market works in a normalized capitalist economy.

When supply goes up, price goes down. When supply goes down, price goes up.

However, it is important to note here that the supply of corporate stock can be affected by not only the number of sellers in the open market but also by the number of shares outstanding.

For example, a company may decide to issue new stock to the public which increases total supply. Usually, this action has a negative effect on price.

Alternatively, if a company decides to buy-back some of its own stock, the number of shares available in the open market will decrease and thus reduce the total supply that can be traded. This action usually has a positive effect on price.

Companies will generally buy-back stock when share prices are relatively inexpensive and these decisions are often implemented with the goal of driving market valuations higher in the future.

A company's total market value is typically referred to as its market capitalization (or "market cap").

Market Cap can be calculated by multiplying the stock price by the number of shares outstanding.

For example, a company with a share price of $50 and 10 million shares outstanding would have a total market capitalization equal to $500 million.

$50 share price x 10,000,000 shares outstanding = $500,000,000 market cap

Now let us talk about options trading.

Options Trading

Within the context of the GameStop story, it is important to understand options trading as well as the basics of buying and selling stock. So, let us move on.

Unlike stocks, which give buyers actual ownership in the underlying company, options give investors only the *right* (or option as the name suggests) to buy or sell a specific asset (like a stock in our case) at a predetermined price on or before a specific future date.

In every option contract, the buyer will set a predetermined expiration date and stock price that will be used to determine the outcome of the position.

The expiration date is often referred to as the "trade expiry" or "time to maturity" and the stock price is typically referred to as the "strike price."

These days, most call option contracts in retail markets are purchased through online brokerages and the positions can often be updated (or "rolled") later if adjustments need to be made.

For investors who believe a stock is going up, "call" options are generally used. In these situations, investors are betting that on or before the expiration of the contract, the price of the stock is going to be higher than the price at which they will have the right to buy it.

In other words, they are buying the right to buy at a discount, so to speak.

Profits are made when the investor chooses to exercise the call option and purchase the stock at the discounted rate, so to speak, and then sold on the open market for a higher price.

It is important to note here that investors are not required to exercise call options. In the case when an investor is wrong, and a stock price drops below the strike price of the call option, losses are therefore limited to the original price paid for the options contract (also known as the "option premium").

In this way, options trading differentiates itself further from traditional stock trading. The maximum potential loss in any option trade is limited and clearly defined even before the position is triggered.

Overall, this shows that while there is a certain level of risk that is commonly associated with options trading, it should be noted that the risks are limited and predefined.

As an example, let us assume that we are interested in buying a call option that gives investors the opportunity to buy 100 shares of Apple (NASDAQ: AAPL) at a strike price of $125 using a time that is three months in the future (which represents the time to maturity). The cost of the trade (which is the price of the option contract) will rise if the underlying stock valuation increases.

However, the cost of the trade will fall if the underlying stock value declines.

After purchasing this contract, one can hold the position until the final maturity period or sell the position if market conditions suggest that an exit is prudent. If we hold the position until the expiration date, we will officially take delivery of 100 shares of AAPL at a price of $125 per share.

Of course, this share price will be available even if the market price on the stock is much higher. Let us assume that bullish trends in APPL stock sent share prices to $165 during the three-month period of our position.

Since the current market price is above the strike price, individual share price profits will be equal to the new valuation ($165) minus the option contract's strike price ($125) and its premium (which varies depending on the trading broker and market conditions). We would then multiply this figure by 100 (since this is the number of shares originally defined in the option contract) to determine the total profit on the trade.

OK. That is enough about call options.

Now let us talk briefly about put options.

In contrast to call options, which give investors the right to *buy* at a certain price at a certain time in the future, a "put" option is a bearish trading contract that gives investors the right to *sell* at a certain price at a certain time in the future. In short, a put option is purchased because the investor believes a stock is going down to a level that is at or below a specific price on or before a specific date in the future (usually within 3 months).

As a result, the value of a put options contract will *increase* when stock prices do in fact decline (or when interest rates drop). Conversely, put options *decrease* in value when share prices move higher (or when a contract's time to maturity draws closer).

Like a call option, a put option is not required to be exercised. Therefore, the maximum amount of money that can be lost on a put option contract is limited to the amount paid for the contract (also known as the contract premium).

Let us review. A call option is used when an investor believes a stock price is going up. A put option is used when an investor believes a stock price is going down.

Call, up. Put, down.

More importantly, we have learned that there are multiple types of trading instruments that can be used to profit in both bullish and bearish market conditions.

When an investor believes a stock price or market is going down, another type of trade that can be initiated is called a short sale. Here we introduce the concept of short selling.

Short Selling

Adam Hayes who writes for *Investopedia* provides this definition of traditional short selling:

"Short selling occurs when an investor borrows a security and sells it on the open market, planning to buy it back later for less money. Short sellers bet on, and profit from, a drop in a security's price. This can be contrasted with long investors who want the price to go up." (Hayes, 2021)

As you can see from this simple definition, short selling carries extremely high risk. If an investor initiates a short trade on a stock but share prices rise instead of fall after the trade is initiated, the trader is forced to buy back shares at the higher price levels to pay back (or settle) what was borrowed. Since there is no limit to the amount a stock price can move up, the potential for loss is infinite.

In contrast, as we discussed above, potential loss from a put option is limited to the amount that is initially paid by the investor to open the trade.

Therefore, while put options and short sales are both bearish types of trades, the varying level of associated risk is critically different.

For example, let us assume that we buy a three-month put option in MSFT stock using a strike price of $235 per share. In this case, we will need to see the stock decline in value to reach profitability in the position. If the stock instead makes an unexpected bullish move to let us say $285 per share after a positive earnings report during this period, we will simply not exercise our put option (or right to sell) and the most we will lose would be equal to the amount we paid to purchase the contract (which is usually negligible, on a relative basis).

However, if we had adopted a simple short position as opposed to purchasing a put option, we would be liable for losses of roughly $5,000 on a trade worth 100 shares. In this example, it is not difficult to see why a relatively small premium on an option contract would be much cheaper than the losses that would accumulate if we were to adopt an outright short position.

Understanding the high level of risk associated with short selling is imperative within the context of the GameStop story.

In addition to being highly risky, it is important to note here that shorting a stock in high volume (volume that can usually be achieved only by institutional investors) drives the price of the stock down. Because of this, it is easy to see why this trading strategy is also controversial as well as risky.

As Elon Musk famously tweeted on January 28th, 2021: *"u can't sell houses u don't own, u can't sell cars u don't own, but u *can* sell stock u don't own!? this is bs – shorting is a scam legal only for vestigial reasons"*

What is a short squeeze?

Of course, the GameStop story is composed of quite a lot of technical jargon and market terminology that might be unfamiliar to readers with limited investment experience. But now that we understand that investors can profit from both positive and negative market trends, we should also understand how some of those strategies can backfire. This will require an explanation of one more piece of investment terminology that will prove to be critical when we discuss the surge in share prices that would ultimately be seen in shares of GameStop stock during the January 2021 trading period.

While there are many unique factors within this narrative that are almost entirely unprecedented in the history of the financial markets, the concept of the "short-squeeze" has been one of the most heavily discussed terms in the media coverage. A short-squeeze describes a relatively common occurrence that has long been around within the context of short-selling itself. While most participants in the stock market are focused on buy-and-hold strategies (which benefit when share prices rise in value), Wall Street hedge funds have access to a broad array of creative tactics that can be used to speculate on stock price movements travelling in any direction.

As we discussed earlier, short selling requires an investor to borrow shares of stock when they believe that valuations are likely to decline in the future. If these expectations turn out to be accurate, these bearish investors can buy back those shares (at a cheaper price) and profit from the negative difference. But if those expectations turn out to be incorrect (and share prices rise after the short trade is initiated), those bearish traders are forced to buy back shares at higher price levels. Since investors must pay the difference between the trade's opening and closing prices, this outcome results in losses for the position. Additionally, short positions always come with an expiration date so when share prices rise unexpectedly, short sellers are often forced to react quickly to limit losses.

Unexpected spikes in share prices will usually amount to the "worst case scenario" for investors that are trading on the short side of the market. Often, this scenario causes a mass exodus of investors looking to close-out their short-sell positions. Essentially, this activity creates an influx of long new positions in the market because bearish investors are buying back shares as the short trades are closed. When these events are significant enough to generate a dominant surge in buying activity, the result is a "short-squeeze" that sends share prices higher.

As the saying goes, the unexpected buying activity "squeezes" the market's short sellers out of their positions and many of these bearish investors are likely to encounter trading losses along the way. Historical examples of this type of activity were seen when shares of Tesla, Inc. (NASDAQ: TSLA) attracted a large amount of short interest in early 2020. In this case, bearish investors saw the stock as overvalued, and they bet against the market's growing enthusiasm as it related to Tesla's still-unproven ability to surpass traditional automakers and sell electric vehicles to mainstream consumers.

During this period, TSLA became the most heavily shorted stock in the United States (with nearly 20% of Tesla's outstanding stock being sold short by investors). However, continued gains in share prices gradually forced bearish investors to exit their positions and this quickly resulted in gains of roughly 400% relative to the stock's market valuation near the end of 2019. Ultimately, these events resulted in incredible losses of $40 billion for the short-selling community and shares of TSLA went on to record annual gains of 743% for the full-year period in 2020.

As we can see, short squeezes can occur because many bearish traders establish positions based on the belief that a stock's valuation will decline in the future. However, these expectations can be rattled when a positive earnings performance or favorable news story changes the outlook and inspires an even larger number of traders to establish long positions in the stock. In some cases, the turnaround in share prices might only be a temporary event. But if the oncoming bullish price movements are sizable enough, they can force short sellers to take cover and close-out their positions to avoid further losses.

As a protective measure, the best way of identifying whether a stock is likely to encounter a short squeeze in the future would be to analyze its short interest level (which measures the percentage of shares sold short relative to the number of shares outstanding).

An even more advanced approach would be to analyze the stock's short interest ratio (which divides the number of shares sold short by the average trading volume each day). In both cases, a higher figure indicates greater risk for a potential short squeeze in the stock. This analysis can also be used as a proxy to determine likely volatility levels in any equity market investment.

As we will see in our study of the historic GameStop short-squeeze, speculative stocks in the small-cap category are often characterized by higher levels of short interest when compared to larger companies. But relative changes in a stock's short interest levels can be viewed as an essential indicator of whether the market's view is changing on the outlook for a given company.

For example, a stock that typically encounters short interest levels of 20-40% might see significant changes in share price if short interest rises above (or moves below) that historical range.

Rising short interest often indicates greater levels of pessimism in the market (which can depress share prices). But if these levels reach excessive levels, the stock will become increasingly vulnerable to the possibility of a short squeeze (which could lead to a dramatic rally in share prices).

Conversely, falling short interest indicates improved optimism in the market (which generally sends share prices higher) and this reduces the probability that a stock will encounter a short squeeze in the future.

What is Market Manipulation?

Market manipulation is illegal in the United States and is defined by the US Securities Exchange Act as "transactions which create an artificial price or maintain an artificial price for a tradable security" (Wikipedia, n.d.). In other words, any action taken by an investor to unfairly influence the price of an asset with the intention of profiting from the price fluctuation is considered market manipulation. In most cases, market manipulation is difficult to accomplish when the size of a company being targeted falls into "large-cap" status (In general, "large-cap" refers to companies with a market cap above $10 billion[1]). However, "small-cap" or "micro-cap" stocks, like GameStop for example, can be vulnerable targets for illegal market manipulation since these stocks typically fall under the radar of the analyst community and are rarely covered by the financial news media.

Because of this, many critics questioned whether the excessive short strategies used by some Wall Street hedge funds against a struggling, small-cap stock violated the "spirit of the law" since those strategies could have artificially deflated share prices.

However, no specific charges were levied against any of Wall Street's bearish entities with an interest in GameStop during the period that led up to the unprecedented volatility in the stock.

CHAPTER 3

The Reddit Rebellion

Now, we get to the parts of the story that are truly revolutionary in nature. If we look at the long-term history of the financial markets, most of the dominant players using short strategies were the institutional investors working in hedge funds on Wall Street. While anyone might be technically capable of shorting a stock, the reality is that many smaller investors might not even know what "short-selling" is. Furthermore, smaller traders in the markets lack access to the capital required to mount a suitable defense against the much larger investing entities that are consistently active when shorting equities.

In the GameStop story, an online group of contrarian traders looked for stocks characterized by high levels of short interest among Wall Street's hedge funds. As part of a strategy to exploit the growing possibility that the investing establishment would fall victim to the effects of a massive, short-squeeze, traders frequenting a discussion forum on Reddit called WallStreetBets (r/WallStreetBets) analyzed GameStop's short interest levels and determined that heavy one-sided positioning for the stock exposed critical vulnerabilities among institutional investors.

Clearly, two sides emerged as the major players during these events. On one side, we had the institutional establishment as it is embodied by hedge funds working on Wall Street. On the other side, we have a group of individual traders communicating through Reddit's social media platform and adopting contrarian strategies in stocks that were largely forgotten by the market. Surprisingly, this latter group managed to wield a high level of power that was completely unexpected and took most members of the financial analysis community off-guard.

Before long, the financial news media outlets began to refer to these individual investors operating outside of the realms of Wall Street as "retail traders." Essentially, this vaguely condescending term refers to non-professional traders that execute positions using online brokerage companies or other types of secondary investment accounts. Since these traders are not viewed as having "direct access" to the market (and often invest using accounts that are relatively small in terms of dollar-value), they are often viewed as being less consequential in terms of the impact their positions can have on market prices.

In contrast, the umbrella term "institutional investors" refers to entities (usually professional portfolio managers or hedge funds) that initiate large-scale investments and often operate in upscale regional locations (such as Lower Manhattan, Tokyo, or London) to gain better access to wealthy clients. Since the large position sizes executed by institutional investors tend to group together enormous pools of assets, the total effect institutional positions can have on the market is generally viewed as substantial.

As a way of combating some of these disadvantages, the Securities and Exchange Commission (SEC) has delineated goals designed to protect retail investors from predatory brokerage practices and to ensure orderly functions in financial markets. For these reasons, the SEC provides educational materials for retail investors and allocates resources that enforce regulations to promote confidence while ensuring that everyday people feel comfortable investing in the financial markets. (White, n.d.)

However, as we will see in the following pages describing the events of the GameStop saga, this group of small-scale investors is not nearly as weak and defenseless as they may have been in the past.

The rise of the internet over the last two decades has helped level the playing field within the short selling space in some ways, primarily by decentralizing access to information and education as well as providing a multitude of brokerage platforms that anyone can use.

But the Reddit Rebellion demonstrated another way by which the internet can help level the playing field: social media. Undeniably, the group of so-called "retail" investors has proven that they can influence financial markets in powerful ways.

Although the numbers of active trading communities on social media platforms have existed for many years in increasing numbers, the power of these groups to collectively compete with the institutional investors has been unappreciated until now. Tim Collins who writes for RealMoney.com said:

"There's been an awakening. A large group of retail traders have realized if they work together, using market tools such as out-of-the-money call options or low-float stocks, they can overpower any institution or short seller in the world, outside of the Fed, of course." (Collins, 2021)

As larger portions of the global investment community gain access to the trading strategies that benefit from downside activity in the market and pair them with the power of social media, we can reasonably expect that Wall Street's prior dominance in the amount of short-selling activity will diminish over time.

These emerging trends are still in their relative infancy and the recent activities in GameStop stock have revealed the one-sided nature of these practices as they are implemented in global markets.

In January 2021, roughly 140% of GameStop's "public float" (which is a term that refers to the total number of shares currently outstanding) had been sold short. For newer investors, it might seem impossible (or, at least, difficult to imagine) that more than the total number of shares available in the market could have been sold short at any given time. However, this scenario is not necessarily uncommon which suggests that the true power of Wall Street is sometimes incomprehensible and that these scenarios have been particularly ripe for disruption for quite a while.

*A brief note here about the title of this book. You may or may not be asking yourself, "What does stonked mean?" In general, the English word "stonk" is typically used as a verb in military slang which means to bombard with concentrated artillery fire. But like most slang, the word stonk is used in many different ways that have no relation whatsoever to its military roots. For example, sometimes the term is used to refer to a person who is really, really high. Or drunk. Or both.

But within the context of the GameStop story, the word stonk is internet slang used commonly in online trading forums to refer to a stock that is on the move (usually up) for reasons that are humorous or ironic.

The term "meme stock" has a similar meaning. Erin Gobler who writes for The Balance described meme stocks as "stocks that have seen an increase in volume not because of the company's performance, but rather because of hype on social media and online forums like Reddit. For this reason, these stocks often become overvalued, seeing drastic price increases in just a short amount of time."

As a verb in this context, stonked is also used to describe a kind of jab or blow that was dealt to Wall Street by the populist, online trading community.

Refer to meme image below.

Image credit: Chris Politylo

CHAPTER 4

The Timeline of Events

August 2020

For years, GameStop had been a brick-and-mortar staple; an icon within the gaming community. It was, and still is, a place for gamers to buy and trade video games. However, the digital transformation of gaming made it easier and faster to obtain video games by instantly downloading them directly to a game console. This new way of buying threatened the viability of GameStop's brick-and-mortar business model. Many thought it was only a matter of time until this brick-and-mortar superstar would become a thing of the past. In institutional investment circles, jokes about GameStop becoming the next Blockbuster video had become common.

According to Wedbush analyst Michael Pachter, GameStop's physical disc-based gaming model was in major trouble and it would only be a matter of time before the business would likely face its total collapse:

"I definitely think it's a melting ice cube. For sure it is going to go away eventually. And for sure their future will be truncated and eliminated the day that discs stop being manufactured." (Gilbert, 2019)

Unfortunately, this failure to adapt to changing market trends saw GameStop's foot traffic decline by nearly 3% in 2019. The following year (in part due to COVID-19 lockdowns) the retailer saw a massive 27.3% decline in foot traffic.

So in August of 2020, when Ryan Cohen, co-founder of online pet supplies retailer Chewy, Inc. (NYSE: CHWY), disclosed a 5.8 million-share stake in GameStop Corp. (NYSE: GME) in a filing with the Securities and Exchange Commission (SEC), it caught much of the investment community by surprise. This stake represented 9% of GameStop's total market cap. However, Cohen's investment firm did not stop there. To further establish an expanded bullish presence in GameStop, RC Ventures continued buying GME stock in the months that followed. By December of 2020, the firm owned nearly 13% of the video game retailer's total shares outstanding.

During this period of aggressive acquisition, Cohen publicly made the argument that GameStop should move away from its previous reliance on sales from brick-and-mortar stores and focus instead on mobile gaming, e-sports, and digital sales. The entire letter Cohen sent to GameStop's Board of Directors can be read here.

Given Cohen's record of success within the e-commerce space, it is not surprising that this high-stakes bet on GameStop caught the attention of retail traders around the world.

Afterall, shares of Chewy, Cohen's wildly successful e-commerce company, had at the time rallied by nearly 350% in the 13 months prior (from November 2019 to December 2020). These types of outsized returns would make anyone paying attention eager to consider following Cohen's lead. And they did.

Notably, a discussion thread on Reddit referred to as the subreddit WallStreetBets, which is largely comprised of independent retail traders, took up this conversation and ran with it. For many of the group's members, Cohen's announcement brought their attention to a new buying opportunity.

When it was discovered through publicly available data that GME stock was massively shorted by institutional investment firms (for reasons that were obvious to group members), gears were set in motion that began to propel Wall Street and Main Street towards an epic faceoff.

In the months leading up to the December release of GameStop's quarterly earnings report, the price of GME stock rose nearly 230%.

Dec. 8th, 2020:

The bullish momentum of GME stock hit a temporary pause when the company released its quarterly earnings report on December 8th, 2020. The report revealed clear weakness in corporate revenues largely due to store closures during COVID-19 pandemic lockdowns. Additionally, these backward-looking results led to speculation that GameStop was falling behind its competitors in terms of its ability to adapt and capitalize on emerging trends in the digitization of online gaming.

In the following trading session, shares of GME gapped lower to reach session lows of $13.23, which marked a decline of nearly 32% from the highs of the month prior.

From an investment perspective, this event was significant. Online group members of the WallStreetBets trading community saw this dip as another excellent buying opportunity. The price correction did not last long and GME stock continued its upward trajectory.

Jan 11th, 2021:

On January 11th, 2021, GameStop's board appointed Ryan Cohen and two more veterans from the e-commerce arena to its ranks. In essence, this tactical move sent an open signal to the market that GameStop was serious about its commitment to a new digital strategy. However, even as these new strategic announcements were released, short interest on the stock totaled almost 71 million shares which managed to cap GME stock valuations at a mere price of roughly $20. This price cap suggested that institutional investors on Wall Street were failing to take much notice of the company's changing outlook.

It was clear that GME was still one of the most hated stocks in the Wall Street investment community.

But down on Main Street, retail traders within the Reddit trading community saw these weak price valuations as another opportunity to get long GME stock despite the formidable opposition they would face from Wall Street short sellers.

Almost immediately, the net-effect of these bullish trading decisions among the Reddit cohort led to rallies in GME share prices. During the single-session trading period that followed GameStop's announcement to appoint Ryan Cohen to its board, GME stock gained by 12%.

The faceoff between these two buying and selling forces was heating up. The markets were approaching the throes of what would become an historic short-squeeze sending GME stock on its path to surge above $480 per share.

Jan 13th, 2021:

On January 13th, 2021, the gloves were officially off and buying activity amongst the Reddit cohort sent GME share prices higher by 57% in a single session. To put these moves into perspective, this bullish trading activity allowed GME stock to break out of a trading range that lasted nearly 20 years and the size of these gains created the largest single-session rally in the company's history.

Breaking the tradition of buying low and selling high, the Reddit cohorts continued to buy even as share prices skyrocketed. This activity pushed the stock price to a new high of $39.90 during the following trading session (a move that indicated single-day gains of 27%).

As another expression of the strength of what was then being referred to as the Reddit Rebellion, it should be noted that at this point the value of GME stock had surpassed its median analyst price target of $12.50 per share by nearly 220%.

For many investors, these events destroyed some of the most long-standing beliefs in the world of finance. The credibility of Wall Street's opinion on what the appropriate value should be of securities in equity markets was in this case rendered something close to irrelevant.

Also surprising is the fact that the magnitude of these moves had not yet been fully realized. In many ways, these initial rallies in GME share prices served to attract a greater level of attention from the major financial media news outlets. This media attention was arguably the central factor that put this once-forgotten stock back on the map for bullish investors that were ready to drive Game-Stop much, much higher.

Jan 19th, 2021:

Now that the financial news media outlets were on-board and tracking the narrative of this historic story, the Battle Royale being waged between Wall Street's hedge funds (the short sellers) and Reddit's retail traders (the bullish buyers) was seen to be developing in full force.

On January 19th, short-sellers Citron Research fired a Twitter attack against the Reddit cohort which arrogantly called into question the ability of the retail trading community to keep pace with the institutional heavyweights that had dominated the order flow of the financial market since its inception. The tweet read:

"GameStop $GME buyers… are the suckers at this poker game. Stock back to $20 fast. We understand short interest better than you."

To many, this public display of condescension directed at the retail trading community seemed to represent the arrogance of the Wall Street institutional investment class as a whole. In hindsight, the tweet was the gasoline the fire needed to explode.

As a point of reference, GME stock traded within a range of $36-45 per share on the day Citron's incendiary attack was levied against the Reddit trading community.

Unfortunately for Citron Research, the firm found itself on the wrong side of the bet. Just seven trading days later, the historic short squeeze led by the WallStreetBets online trading community would force GME stock to trade at prices 10x higher ($483 per share) than they were when Citron tweeted its attack against the retail trading community.

Three days later, in what can only be described as an act of true comeuppance, Citron Research founder Andrew Left posted a public apology video announcement. The apology was in response to the incendiary tweet he posted just 10 days prior. What follows is an excerpt from the full video that can be seen here:

"20 years ago, I started Citron with the intention of protecting the individual against Wall Street, against the frauds and the stock promotions [that] were just all over. Where we started Citron was supposed to be against the establishment, we have actually become the establishment. So as of today, Citron Research will no longer be publishing what can be considered as short-selling reports."

Public apologies like this, combined with the surging price of GME stock almost out of spite for the big wigs on Wall Street, showed that the Reddit trading community's ability to single-handedly take down the titans of Wall Street had reached a level of strength that was simply undeniable. A new market force had arrived: trading populism.

Jan 22nd, 2021:

Shares of GME posted another 51% in single-session gains on January 22nd. At this stage, it was clear that Wall Street was becoming concerned with the severity of the stock's short-squeeze and trading of GME shares was halted by the SEC (on four separate occasions) due to what was described as "excessive volatility."

According to the U.S. Financial Industry Regulatory Authority (FINRA), the SEC is authorized "to suspend trading in any stock for a period of up to 10 business days... when it believes that the investing public may be at risk." In most cases, this occurs when a company fails to maintain proper filing records for annual or quarterly earnings reports designed to provide adequate information (such as financial performances or the corporate outlook from management) that might be needed for the investing public to make informed trading decisions. Another reason why the SEC might suspend trading of a stock might be when the quality of a company's public information is suspected to be inaccurate.

However, when trading of GME stock was halted by the SEC, it was not because of any of these reasons. Rather, the SEC's decision to halt trading in GameStop shares was based on the stock's uncharacteristic trading volatility and the possibility that market manipulation was what was driving share prices higher. Since no hard evidence of market manipulation was found, shares of GME stock continued trading in the open market and eventually reached a new record high on January 22nd.

Jan 25th, 2021:

As momentum buying continued to propel share prices higher, GameStop stock added gains of as much as 144% during the single-session trading period on January 25th. As questions continued to circulate about the prospects of excess volatility and market manipulation, public trading of GME shares was halted again on nine separate occasions.

On CNBC, Jim Cramer said, "The mechanics of the market are breaking down. ... I've never seen the guns like this. They can break shorts."

For many retail traders, these attempts by the SEC to inhibit buying activity in GME stock violated basic rules of equality in capitalist systems.

Jan 26th, 2021:

On January 26th, 2021, Elon Musk posted his influential tweet: *"Gamestonk!!"* – which included a web link to the WallStreetBets discussion thread on Reddit. In response to the affirmative tweet, WallStreetBets users bestowed the Tesla CEO with a new moniker: "Papa Musk."

As is often the case when Elon Musk offers his stamp of approval on something, the tweet had a bullish effect on share prices and GME closed with gains of 92% on the session. As the volatility continued to rage, trading activity in GME stock was halted yet again on five separate occasions during the January 26th session.

William Galvin, the Secretary of the Commonwealth of Massachusetts, said in a statement to *Barron's*, "This is certainly on my radar. I'm concerned, because it suggests that there is something systemically wrong with the options trading on this stock." (Salzman, 2021)

Jan 27th, 2021:

On January 27th, short-sellers Citron Research and Melvin Capital allegedly closed their bearish positions in GME. With share prices hitting highs of $380 during the session, successful short-squeeze efforts by the r/WallStreetBets community generated substantial losses for institutional traders and hedge funds who had taken massive, short positions on the stock. Moreover, when short trades are closed, they effectively turn into new, long trades (to balance and settle the position).

As a result, major institutional investors were essentially putting new buy orders in the market when they closed their GME short positions. Ultimately, this activity pushed the stock price even higher to levels that few people in the analyst community would have ever thought possible.

By this time, the number of subscribers of the subReddit r/Wall-

StreetBets had grown to 5.2 million. To catch up with the flood of new posts, r/WallStreetBets moderators were even forced to take the forum offline for portions of the trading session. The group was later locked as an "invite-only" page to manage the surging volume of new contributors.

Jan 28th, 2021:

On January 28th, the Robinhood trading platform sparked outrage among its members by restricting further buying of GME stock while continuing to allow the sale of the stock.

Additionally, the trading platform explained that margin requirements would be increased for shares of GameStop which meant that traders would need to provide additional capital to execute larger positions.

Robinhood's message on its website read:

"We continuously monitor the markets and make changes where necessary. Considering recent volatility, we are restricting transactions for certain securities to position closing only."

This development enraged many within the retail trading community and beyond. Among the many suspicious things about this new development was the fact that Robinhood had prevented traders from buying GME shares but not from selling them.

Critics claimed that this one-sided policy, although temporary, created an unfair advantage for hedge funds and institutional investors who had short positions on the stock. Halting the buying of the stock would temporarily stop the price from going any higher while continuing to allow the sale of the stock would theoretically push prices back down. Both outcomes would benefit the institutional short sellers by preventing further losses.

It is important to note here that Robinhood is a relatively new trading platform founded in 2013 with the expressed mission to "provide everyone with access to the financial markets, not just the wealthy". The company planned to accomplish this mission in part by eliminating fees and offering an easy-to-use interface that could be understood by beginner investors. Because of this mission, the trading platform had become quite popular with many of the younger investors in the WallStreetBets community.

So, to the retail trading community it felt like a proverbial stab in the back. From the outside, it looked like Robinhood was not "for the people" after all but rather working for Wall Street in what appeared to be an effort to minimize institutional losses at the expense of the little guys on Main Street. Additionally, the new restrictions appeared to deliberately make it more difficult for the retail trading community to enact coordinated market strategies in general.

In one exchange that was particularly heated, Barstool Sports founder Dave Portnoy (a bullish GME trader that reportedly lost $700,000 trading the stock) went so far as to call Robinhood CEO Vladimir Tenev a "liar" and a "rat" and even suggested that people from the trading brokerage's managerial team should "go to jail" because of their decisions to halt GME order flows from the long side of the market.

Ultimately, no charges were brought against Robinhood's management team, but CEO Tenev was later asked to testify before the U.S. Congress and answer questions about why the company implemented these targeted restrictions on its users. Prior comments from Robinhood have suggested that the firm's trading restrictions were needed to act in compliance with SEC mandates, saying:

"These requirements exist to protect investors and the markets, and we take our responsibilities to comply with them seriously, including through the measures we have taken."

Following Robinhood's announcement to restrict share-buying activities in GameStop, the stock reversed its prior gains and fell from all-time highs (at $483) to hit lows of $112.25 per share (an overall loss of -57.6%) before the end of the volatile January 28th trading session.

Similar restrictions were established through other popular trading brokerages (such as Interactive Brokers).

These decisions to freeze transactions for retail traders while Wall Street's hedge funds continued to trade through its traditional venues is what turned the GameStop saga into a modern version of David vs. Goliath (and led to widespread accusations of market manipulation that disproportionately impacted the platform's own client base).

Jan 29th, 2021:

The following day, Robinhood released a statement explaining that restrictions on its stock trading platform would be eased but that traders would only be allowed to buy one share of GME (and other tickers on its restricted stocks list). Here, it should be noted that no such restrictions were placed on traders' abilities to short the stocks on Robinhood's restricted trading list.

Just prior to the market open on January 29th, the SEC also released a statement-as a warning to various trading brokerages and Reddit users citing potential market manipulation or abusive trading activity:

"The Commission is closely monitoring and evaluating the extreme price volatility of certain stocks' trading prices over the past several days… extreme stock price volatility has the potential to expose investors to rapid and severe losses and undermine market confidence. As always, the Commission will work to protect investors, to maintain fair, orderly, and efficient markets, and to facilitate capital formation.

The Commission is working closely with our regulatory partners, both across the government and at FINRA and other self-regulatory organizations, including the stock exchanges, to ensure that regulated entities uphold their obligations to protect investors and to identify and pursue potential wrongdoing. The Commission will closely review actions taken by regulated entities that may disadvantage investors or otherwise unduly inhibit their ability to trade certain securities."

However, the market appeared to shrug-off these warnings from the SEC and renewed buying activity in GME sent the stock toward intraday highs of $413.98 per share. With single-session gains of 68% on January 29th, shares of GME stock recorded shocking gains of over 400% in just one week. According to market-to-market research from S3 Partners, GameStop's short-sellers were reportedly forced to endure losses of nearly $20 billion in less than a month - even with Robinhood's efforts to calm volatility and prevent Reddit's short-squeeze attack by restricting the platform's ability to purchase shares of GME.

Not to be outdone, Elon Musk added the #Bitcoin hashtag to his Twitter profile on the same day and market valuations of the BTC/USD cryptocurrency pair spiked by 20% (rising by more than $5,000) in the space of an hour. Musk included a cryptic tweet following the volatile GameStop trading session, which simply read:

"In retrospect, it was inevitable."

Overall, Musk's Twitter message seemed to be a fitting conclusion to an incredibly volatile trading week characterized by historic changes that might forever redefine the way retail traders are viewed within the market at large. Ultimately, the "amateur" investors found in the WallStreetBets trading forum were officially able to declare victory against the hedge funds and institutional trading entities that had dominated and influenced trends in equity markets for as long as anybody could realistically remember.

January 31st, 2021:

Elon Musk (who was then being referred to as "Papa Musk" by many of the retail traders within the WallStreetBets community) decided to take matters into his own hands in what turned out to be an impressive work of investigative journalism on his part. To get to the bottom of the controversy, Musk invited Vlad Tenev, CEO of Robinhood to a call on the Clubhouse app. At the time, anyone who had the Clubhouse app could drop in and listen to the live call. Musk's line of questioning was direct and to the point. He asked the questions that needed to be answered. Was Robinhood pressured by the so-called powers-that-be on Wall Street to suspend buying activity on GameStop stock? Was market manipulation involved that would suggest that the stock market is rigged in favor of Wall Street? What follows is the transcript of Musk's interview with the CEO of Robinhood. The full interview can be listened to here:

Elon: Vlad the stock impaler.

Vlad: Hey, guys, thanks for inviting me. It's good to hang with all of you.

Elon: Alright, Vlad. What really happened? Give us the inside scoop.

Vlad: Alright well I was actually hoping that you would invite me up for the fermi paradox part because this has been a very surreal weekend and week for me. One of the really great things is all the people coming out of the woodwork to offer support for the company, offer advice, so I got introduced today and actually I should say I just randomly downloaded Clubhouse a couple days ago just to see what it was all about so this is my first time literally using the app. But, yeah, I uh, I got introduced to your friend Antonio, Elon, who had some good advice for me and then introduced me to you. You had some great advice. And then I figured you know? I heard about this Clubhouse and this has got to be part of the simulation and so I just thought why now? So Here I am. I'm actually an adherent to the Simulation Hypothesis.

Elon: Alright, well. Spill the beans, Man. What happened last week? Why can't people buy the GameStop shares? The people demand an answer, and they want to know the details and the truth.

Vlad: OK so let me start by giving a little bit of background. So I'm the

Chief Executive of Robinhood...

Elon: *Yeah we know, man. Just come on...*

Vlad: *I'll go through this quickly. Don't worry. This is important. Robinhood actually a couple of companies. So there's an introducing broker dealer called Robinhood Financial which is basically the app that you know and love. It processes trades if you're a customer of Robinhood financial.*

Then there's the clearing broker dealer, Robinhood Securities, that clears and settles the trades.

Then we have Robinhood Crypto which is our crypto business. All of these are kind of different entities that are differently operated. So basically Wednesday of last week, we had unprecedented volume, unprecedented load on the system, a lot of these so called [meme] stocks were going viral on social media and people were joining Robinhood and there was a lot of net buy activity on them. As you guys all know and Robinhood at this time was number 1 on the iOS app store and pretty close if not number one on google play as well. So just unprecedented activity, right? So Thursday morning, ok, so I'm sleeping, but at 3:30am pacific our operations team receives a file from the NSCC which is the National Securities Clearing Corporation. So basically as a clearing broker, and this is where Robinhood Securities comes in, we have to put up money to the NSCC based on some factors including the volatility of the trading activity, concentration in certain securities (this is the equities business so it's based on stock trading, not options trading or anything else) so they gave us a file with the deposit and the request was around $3b which is an order of magnitude more than what it typically is, right?

Elon: *Now why was that so high? It sounds like an unprecedented increase in demand for capital. What formula did they use to calculate that?*

Vlad: *Well, to give context to that number Robinhood up until that point had raised about $2 billion dollars total in venture capital up* until now. So it's a big number. 3 billion dollars is a large number, right? So basically, we don't have the full details of how that number is calculated, it's a little bit of an opaque formula but there's a component called the VAR (value at risk). That's based on some fairly quantitative things although it's not fully transparent, there are ways to reverse engineer it, but it's not publicly shared. And there is a special component which is discretionary so that kind of acts as a multiplier. And basically...

Elon: *Discretionary? You mean "discretionary" like it's just their opinion?*

Vlad: *Yeah it's a little bit, I mean I'm sure there's definitely more than just their opinion but basically it's based upon growth....*

Elon: *I guess what everyone wants to know is, did something maybe shady go down here? It seems weird that you would get a sudden 3 billion demand at 3:30 in the morning. Just suddenly out of nowhere.*

Vlad: *I wouldn't impute shadiness to it and actually you know the NSCC was reasonable subsequent to this and they worked with us to actually lower it. It was unprecedented activity, and I don't have the full context of what was going on in the NSCC to make these calculations.*

Elon: *Is anyone holding you hostage right now?*

Vlad: *Uh, ha no. no. I'm OK.*

Elon: *Blink twice.*

Vlad: *Ha, yeah, thanks for asking but anyway so this was obviously nerve wracking and I actually was asleep at this time. The operations team was fielding this at 3am and then we got back, put our heads together, our Chief Operating Officer said look let's call up the higher ups at the NSCC to see what's going on. Maybe there's some way we can work with them. So, basically there was another call and they lowered it to something like $1.4 billion dollars from $3. So OK we were making some progress, right? But it's still a high number. And then we* basically proposed, well let's explain to them how we will manage risk in these symbols throughout the day. We proposed marking these volatile stocks that were driving the activity position closing only.

And then at about an hour before market open around 5:30 or 5:00 in the morning, they came back and said that the deposit was $700 million which we then deposited and paid promptly. And then everything was fine. So, that essentially explains why we had to mark these symbols position closing only. And, also why, you know, we knew this was a bad outcome for customers. Part of what has been really difficult is that Robinhood stands for democratizing access to stocks and we want to get people the access, so that has been very challenging. But we had no choice in this case. We had to conform to our regulatory capital requirements and so our team did what we could to make sure that we were available for customers.

Elon: Who controls the NSCC?

Vlad: It's a consortium. It's not quite a government agency. I don't really know the details of all that. And to be fair, I think there was legitimate turmoil in the market. These are unprecedented events with these meme stocks and there was a lot of activity so there probably is some amount of extra risk in the system that warrants higher requirements. So, it's not entirely unreasonable. But we did operational processes to make sure that customers that had positions could sell their open positions because obviously restricting someone, we got a lot of questions about "OK you had to restrict buying why didn't you also restrict selling?" and the fact of the matter is that people get really pissed off if they're holding stock and they want to sell it and they can't. that is categorically worse. And lots of other brokers I think were in the same situation. But Robinhood was in the news but you sort of heard this industry wide, right? Other brokers basically restricted the same exact activity.

Elon: Alright so it sounds like this organization calls you up and they basically have a gun to your head either hand over this money or else. So basically what people are wondering is did you sell your clients down the river or did you have no choice? And if you had no choice then that's understandable. But then we need to find out why you had no choice and who are these people who are saying you have no choice?

Vlad: Yeah, I think that's fair. We have to comply with these requirements, financial institutions have requirements. The formula behind these requirements I think it would obviously be ideal if there was a little bit more transparency so we could plan better around that. But to be fair, we were able to open and serve our customers and 24 hours later our team raised over $1 billion dollars in capital so that when we open tomorrow morning, we'll be able to relax the stringent position limits that we put on these securities on Friday.

Elon: Will there be any limits?

Vlad: Well, I think there's always going to be some theoretical limit because we don't have infinite capital, right? And on Friday there were limits, so there's always going to have to be some limit. I think the question is, will the limits be high enough to the point where they won't impact 99.99 percent of customers. But if someone were to deposit 100 billion dollars and decide to trade in one stock that would not be possible.

Elon: I guess the people want to know whoever put the gun to your head should be willing to answer to the public.

Vlad: Yeah, listen, I know there's processes, this is unprecedented times, and to be fair to those guys they've been reasonable. So, I think the one thing that's maybe not clear to people is that Robinhood is a participant in the financial system so we have to work with all of these counter parties so we do get a lot of questions like why we work with market makers, why we work with clearing houses, it's hard enough to build a introducing a clearing broker dealer not too many people have done that. But the financial system that allows customers to trade shares is sort of complex web of multiple parties and everyone says it could be better, it could be improved, but it's just a necessity of trading equities in the US that you have to do all of these things.

Elon: *Alright, to what degree are you beholden to Citadel?*

Vlad: *So there was a rumor that Citadel or other market makers pressured us into doing this and that's just false, right? Market makers execute our trades, they execute trades of every broker dealer, but this was a clearing house decision, and it was just based on the capital requirements. From our perspective, Citadel and other market makers weren't involved in that.*

Elon: *But wouldn't they have a strong say in who got put in charge of that organization since it's an industry consortium and not a government regulatory agency?*

Vlad: *I don't have any reason to believe that. I think that's just kind of getting into the conspiracy theories a little bit. So I have no reason to believe that that's the case.*

Elon: *Ok. Alright. Well I guess we'll see what happens with future actions. Hopefully that was insightful if not entertaining. Are you not entertained?*

Feb 1st, 2021:

Following what was easily the most turbulent month in GameStop's history as a publicly traded company, Robinhood found itself in a mode of full-on damage control and in dire need of additional funding from its stakeholders. Just days after investment firms Ribbit Capital and Sequoia Capital secured $1 billion in funding for the no-fee trading brokerage firm, another group of existing investors (including Index Ventures, Andreessen Horowitz, ICONIQ, and NEA) raised $2.4 billion in additional capital to help support Robinhood's strained operations.

After momentum-fueled buying interest in GameStop shares skyrocketed, Robinhood's platform systems were under tremendous pressure due to the excessive trading volume and unprecedented order flows stemming from January's events. Additionally, the company faced heightened scrutiny from politicians and social media celebrities focusing on the perception of unequal trading policies that favored institutional investors above Robinhood's retail customer base. As a result, the firm found itself in need of tactical strategies to stop the bleeding while maintaining accordance with the SEC's demands for transparency.

Feb 2nd, 2021:

On February 2nd, 2021, U.S. Treasury Secretary Janet Yellen called a meeting with prominent financial regulators to discuss the events surrounding GameStop stock and their potential long-term effects on market volatility. The meeting included key figures from the SEC, Federal Reserve, and the Commodity Futures Trading Commission (CFTC). In a statement to Reuters, Treasury spokeswoman Alexandra LaManna explained:

"Secretary Yellen believes the integrity of markets is important and has asked for a discussion of recent volatility in financial markets and whether recent activities are consistent with investor protection and fair and efficient markets."

In broad terms, the meeting revealed growing concerns being felt at the highest levels of government as they related to unexpected spikes in short-term stock volatility. The meeting was clearly designed to expedite a review of the regulatory compliance among non-bank investment firms.

With a targeted focus on the stock symbols discussed in Reddit's WallStreetBets forums, the U.S. Treasury Department's regulatory review took a hard look at Citadel (and other short-selling firms) to better understand the role these entities played in driving erratic financial market price movements and assess the extent to which coordinated trading decisions might have had a detrimental impact on unsuspecting investors.

Feb 4th, 2021:

On February 4th, Robinhood gave in to mounting pressures and removed all its trading restrictions in a capitulation move which allowed its platform users to freely enter long positions (of any lot size) in GameStop stock. At this stage, market valuations in GME had returned to levels that were roughly comparable to the price levels leading up to the periods of extreme trading volatility from January 26th to February 2nd.

However, substantial buying activity did re-emerge once Robinhood users were able to freely execute long positions and this helped shares of GME reach highs of $95 during the following trading session. Intraday traders looking to capitalize on short-term price fluctuations quickly took profits into the strength of these rallies and the stock settled at $63.77 (with single-session gains of 19.2%) on February 5th. For the next two weeks, the stock traded in a much tighter price range (roughly $35-60 per share) as investors waited for the next development likely to guide trends in market valuations.

Feb 18th 2021:

On February 18th, the U.S. House Committee on Financial Services held a hearing titled "Game Stopped? Who Wins and Loses When Short-Sellers, Social Media, and Retail Investors Collide" In a virtual setting, Vlad Tenev and other central figures in the GameStop saga were scheduled to give Congressional testimony detailing the events that would become the historic short-squeeze in GameStop stock.

At the hearing, Vlad Tenev defended prior decisions to restrict trading in shares of GameStop stock and said that allegations suggesting Robinhood acted to help institutional investors and hedge funds were "absolutely false". He went on to say:

"The buying surge that occurred during the last week of January in stocks like GameStop was unprecedented, and it highlighted a number of issues that are worthy of deep analysis and discussion."

According to Tenev, the "historic volatility" present in the market during these periods left Robinhood with no choice but to halt trading activity in GME shares. Essentially, trading platforms like Robinhood are required to deposit their own funds through clearing houses until trading orders are fully settled between sellers and buyers. In practice, these actions are designed to cover potential risks if unexpected market volatility creates excessive losses before trades are fully settled.

In the hearing, Tenev explained that on January 28th, Robinhood's clearing house (the National Securities Clearing Corporation, or NSCC) reported a deposit deficit of roughly $3 billion. This marked a substantial increase from the $124 million deficit that was reported in the days leading up to the GameStop short squeeze. For these reasons, Tenev argued that Robinhood had no choice but to restrict trading in the stock tickers discussed in the WallStreetBets subReddit so that the company could raise additional funding.

After $3.4 billion in funding had been secured by February 1st (with the combined investments from Ribbit Capital, Index Ventures, Andreessen Horowitz, Sequoia Capital, ICONIQ, and NEA), Robinhood resumed operations and allowed investors to purchase shares of GameStop stock without restriction.

However, at this stage, many would argue that the damage had already been done. In an open letter to the House committee, the head of the American Securities Association (Christopher Lacovella) dismissed Robinhood's explanations aimed at justifying its restrictive trading policies, saying:

"As the GME short squeeze unfolded, the clearinghouse recognized that an inadequately capitalized broker-dealer could pose a risk to our markets... Attempts to blame the clearing house or the timing of the settlement cycle for what happened during the short squeeze are a smokescreen."

Ultimately, the resulting firestorm of accusations that came from both Democrats and Republicans in Washington suggested that Robinhood implemented policies which backed hedge funds on the wrong side of a losing trade while enacting platform restrictions that disproportionately impacted smaller investors in the retail community. Essentially, this suggests upcoming legislation from the U.S. Congress is likely so that similar events are prevented from happening again in the future.

CHAPTER 5

Irrational Exuberance or Something Else?

Irrational exuberance in the stock market is not new. It is a term frequently used within the context of speculative investing to describe some asset or class that is likely to be greatly overvalued. Although Alan Greenspan coined the term, Robert J. Shiller wrote the book on it, literally. Let us revisit the definition that Shiller gave us in his 2000 publication. Shiller writes,

"Irrational exuberance is the psychological basis of a speculative bubble. I define a speculative bubble as a situation in which news of price increases spurs investor enthusiasm, which spreads by psychological contagion from person to person, in the process amplifying stories that might justify the price increases, and bringing in a larger and larger class of investors who, despite doubts about the real value of an investment, are drawn to it partly by envy of others' successes and partly through a gamblers' excitement. (Shiller, 2000)

The stock market has seen its share of bubbles pop and shorts squeezed. But what is exceptional about the GameStop story is that the exuberance among the buyers was neither irrational nor merely driven by a desire for big gains. Rather, it appeared to be an organized form of protest among people who cared more about dealing damage to Wall Street than about losing their own hard-earned money in the process (when the bubble was destined to pop, of course). The GameStop phenomenon was not merely irrational exuberance; it was the birth of a new way of challenging the status quo: Trading Populism.

Derek Thompson of *The Atlantic* described the GameStop saga well when he wrote:

"A ludicrous stock mania born of pandemic boredom and FOMO, piggybacking off of a clever Reddit revenge plot, which targeted hedge funds, who made a reckless bet on a struggling retailer—and it's going to end with lots of people losing incredible amounts of money." (Thompson, 2021)

In many ways, the GameStop story can be viewed as a fable for the modern age: A group of overlooked, inconsequential investors joined together to take-on the avarice and excess that has characterized the Wall Street hedge fund community since its inception. In the end, Reddit's social trading revolution challenged nearly every aspect of market norms and changed the balance of power in ways that nobody could have anticipated just a short time ago. According to David Sekera, (Morningstar's chief U.S. market strategist):

"The days of equity research limited to the large, bulge-bracket Wall Street firms is long past."

Digital democratization has enabled investors (of all account sizes) to access relevant information in real-time, organize through like-minded social media communities, and make investment decisions capable of carrying the same weight as any large financial institution.

As a greater number of investors learn the new system, the traditional power structure will continue to encounter disruptions in favor of greater technological democratization. Similar sentiments were expressed by Jason Wilkinson (a WallStreetBets trader that turned to Reddit after being fired by his employer near the start of the pandemic):

"Some of the people who are on the [WallStreetBets] thread are probably on par with the stock pickers of these hedge funds. It's knowing

how to know who to listen to —and who to ignore. It's really just a bunch of people sharing ideas. It's the same thing as when Jim Cramer gets on CNBC smashing buttons."

Of course, some social media traders have goals that are quite different from the investment aims of others. As a result, it can be difficult to differentiate between disruptive traders that are investing based on moral reasoning from those that can identify high-probability investment opportunities on a consistent basis. According to market analyst Neil Wilson, some of GameStop's Reddit traders adopted a "vigilante" mindset that was characterized by a targeted focus to attack the Wall Street establishment:

"They had a peculiar vigilante morality that seemed hell-bent on taking on Wall Street. They seem to hate hedge funds and threads are peppered with insults about 'boomer' money. It's a generational fight, redistributive —and all about robbing the rich to give to the millennial 'poor'."

In this case, one thing is certain — in just a matter of weeks the balance of power in the world of finance has shifted in ways that are undeniable and almost totally unexpected. For these reasons, it also seems clear that tactical market trading in the global equities space will likely never be the same again.

CHAPTER 6

Bi-Partisan Unity

In the aftermath of the highly controversial decision to block retail traders from buying GameStop shares while wild price fluctuations were hammering hedge funds with short positions in the stock, further evidence of democratization and unity came in the form of an unexpected bi-partisan agreement to investigate allegations of wrongdoing filed against Robinhood Markets, Inc. From the progressivism of the left to populism of the right, politicians from both sides of the aisle were relatively quick to side with the mostly younger generation of traders looking to disrupt the traditional financial system and usher in a new era of wealth equality through social investment.

In one highly publicized example, Republican Senator Ted Cruz of Texas and Democratic Congresswoman Alexandria Ocasio-Cortez of New York were able to find rare common ground in condemning Robinhood and calling for hearings looking into the platform's disproportionate imposition of trading limits on certain groups of investors. In a tweet, Representative Ocasio-Cortez explained that Robinhood's actions were "unacceptable" and that further inquiries into the matter would be necessary:

"This is unacceptable. We now need to know more about Robinhood's decision to block retail investors from purchasing stock while hedge funds are freely able to trade the stock as they see fit. As a member of the Financial Services Committee, I'd support a hearing if necessary.

Inquiries into freezes should not be limited solely to Robinhood. This is a serious matter. Committee investigators should examine any retail services freezing stock purchases in the course of potential investigations - especially those allowing sales, but freezing purchases."

In response to this public call for an investigative hearing, Senator Cruz (a well-noted political adversary previously involved in several heated exchanges with Ocasio-Cortez) re-tweeted the message and succinctly said: "Fully agree." In practical terms, this extraordinary instance of political unity showed that legislators across the spectrum recognized the need to address inefficiencies in a global financial system that typically favor the largest players in the game.

Similar sentiments were expressed by Republican Senator Marsha Blackburn of Tennessee, who responded to the events on Twitter by saying: "Free the traders on Robinhood." In another tweet showing evidence of unity between the two parties, Democratic Congresswoman Rashida Tlaib of Michigan (a noted member of "The Squad," along with Representative Ocasio-Cortez) renewed demands calling for an investigation into Robinhood's trading practices and the decision to restrict trading of GameStop shares. Blackburn tweeted:

"This is beyond absurd. We need to have a hearing on Robinhood's market manipulation. They're blocking the ability to trade to protect Wall Street hedge funds, stealing millions of dollars from their users to protect people who've used the stock market as a casino for decades."

As calls for increased regulations on Wall Street gained in momentum, it quickly became clear that a rising undercurrent of institutional distrust had resulted from long-term grievances held by those in the retail investment community.

Despite the high level of bi-partisan agreement that seems to exist within the U.S. government, there is little reason to believe that these feelings of injustice and discontent will be ending any time soon. In an environment where most major stock benchmarks trade near all-time highs while the U.S. unemployment rate remains elevated, the extreme divergences between Main Street and Wall Street make it easy to see how growing segments of the population are feeling a sense of injustice and frustration. Given the weakened state of the global economy in the post-pandemic era, most analysts believe financial hardships are likely to continue for an extended period.

In many ways, this recalls the sentiments that were felt during the 2008 financial crisis (when 10 million Americans lost their homes) and we can remember that the following political periods ultimately gave rise to the Tea Party movement of the right and the Occupy Wall Street movement of the left. But while Reddit's attack on Wall Street might not have specific political catalysts on either side, ensuing bi-partisan efforts that have been seen within the highest levels of government reflect the truly populist nature of the GameStop saga and its long-term impact on the totality of the financial markets. According to Republican Newt Gingrich (Speaker of the House during the Clinton administration):

"It's not about Republicans and Democrats. It is lots and lots of normal, everyday people who began to figure out they really got ripped off for the last year just like they got ripped off in 2008 and 2009. What you are seeing is an almost spontaneous cultural reaction in which the little guys and gals are getting together and going after the bigs, so the bigs are having to rig the game in order to survive."

In 2008, a government bailout package worth $700 billion made it possible for the big banks to continue to stay in business but none of the top executives responsible for orchestrating the historic financial collapse were ever prosecuted for their reckless actions. Residual anger driven by resulting populist fervor remained apparent for more than a decade and it was within this context that the Tea Party movement began to gain momentum. In 2010, the Republicans gained control of the House of Representatives while the Democrats faced a backlash from liberal protestors concerned about the issue of economic inequality (which ultimately led to the Occupy Wall Street movement).

Given the unfavorable outcome of these prior events, it seems unlikely that the hedge funds on the wrong side of the GameStop trade will receive much support or sympathy from the policymakers currently residing in Washington. These days, Congress appears to be less receptive to the concerns of institutional investors on Wall Street and instead might choose to capitalize on recent events to advance populist agendas that favor the retail trading community. According to Republican strategist Josh Holmes (advisor to Mitch McConnel, Senator from Kentucky):

"There's a ton of political currency in holding hedge funds' feet to the fire from Democrats and Republicans. If you're sitting on Wall Street looking at this, dismissing people as folks who don't understand the way that the markets work, I think you're going to be in a lot of trouble."

For politicians on both sides of the aisle, the recent market upheaval that has been inspired by the GameStop story can be viewed as a referendum on the institutional elitism that has characterized Wall Street from the very beginning. Bi-partisan agreements to tighten regulatory requirements and punish long-standing practices of corporate greed appear to be much more likely given the ways Republicans and Democrats have already responded to the restrictive decisions implemented by Robinhood and other brokerages. According to Republican Congressman Jeff Fortenberry of Nebraska:

"Big Hedge, with outposts in South Hedge-i-stan (Wall Street) and North Hedge-i-stan (Greenwich, CT), has made trillions shorting great American companies facing a rough patch. Now they are getting a comeuppance from flash mobs of day traders and are paying dearly."

Even moderates and political centrists seem to be taking a decisive stance in suggesting that Robinhood (and other trading brokerages) engaged in practices that protected hedge funds and institutional investors at the expense of the retail trading community. One example of a moderate lawmaker that has adopted this stance is Republican Pat Toomey (Senator from Pennsylvania) who, coincidentally, is set to be appointed as the party leader in the Senate Banking Committee. Senator Toomey recently voiced his concerns and cited Robinhood's lack of transparency following the decisions to restrict retail trading activity on its platform:

"I find it disturbing when retail investors who are simply seeking to buy a stock are frozen out of the market. Retail investors should be free to purchase even highly speculative stocks, just as hedge funds should be free to short them."

CHAPTER 7

The Cryptocurrency Connection

Following the January 28th, 2021 trading session (which is when GME stock skyrocketed to record highs of $483 per share), market valuations for cryptocurrency assets began to see another upswell in buying activity. For example, the market price of bitcoin versus the U.S. dollar (represented by the BTC-USD crypto pair) reversed course from prior lows (near $30,200) and began to rally for most of the following month. On February 21st, market valuations in BTC-USD surged to a new record high (just below $58,400) in a move indicating gains of more than 93% in roughly three-and-a-half weeks.

As a point of reference, the central U.S. stock benchmark (S&P 500) declined by -3.2% during this period and this negative activity shows that bitcoin valuations were able to push against the dominant bearish trends that were seen throughout most of the market. However, this bullish buying activity was not isolated to the bitcoin space and strong upward moves were also seen in the cryptocurrency market's top altcoins. For example, market valuations in Ethereum rallied by 67.3% during this period (as indicated by the ETH-USD cryptocurrency pair). Overall, this shows that the crypto optimism went beyond bitcoin in terms of the space's reach into digitally democratized markets.

Of course, bitcoin and Ethereum are two names that might be familiar to many investors that are without exposure to cryptocurrencies, so it might not be surprising to see these assets move higher on any given day. However, the binance coin (represented by the BNB-USD cryptocurrency pairing) saw bullish moves that were much more substantial in nature. Specifically, the BNB-USD pairing surged by nearly 760% during the trading period that stretched from January 28th to February 19th, and so these moves even managed to outpace all the highly publicized bullishness in bitcoin markets that was reported at the time.

Lesser-known altcoins were also beneficiaries of the retail trading optimism that surrounded the early developments of the GameStop saga. Another example can be found in Cardano (represented by the ADA-USD crypto pair), which gained more than 385% during the month that followed the record highs in GME stock. Additionally, the Litecoin cryptocurrency (represented by the LTC-USD crypto pair) beat bitcoin's performance (with January-February 2021 gains of 104%) and the polka dot cryptocurrency saw gains of 182% (more than doubling the gains of bitcoin during this trading period).

For the most part, these impressive rallies were under-reported by the financial news media outlets and this might have been because so many of Wall Street's analyst community was caught off-guard by the unprecedented story in GameStop. However, a deeper look into the most significant trends that were developing at the time suggests that the ability of retail traders to shift the narrative in favor of social trading and investment democratization went far beyond one or two meme stocks mentioned by the r/WallStreetBets community.

> *For these reasons, a growing number of market analysts have started to explain that there is an underlying connection between GameStop's recent developments and the rising price valuations in cryptocurrency markets. Specifically, the deep distrust of centralized finance as it has been traditionally*

implemented through government entities has only served to add momentum to the widespread adoption of cryptocurrency."

Of course, many of these sentiments are likely based on the underlying characteristics which define the central utilities of cryptocurrency as it exists within the open market.

In many cases, investors that have a longer history of experience trading in the financial markets will have a difficult time accepting coincidences when they become apparent in multiple asset classes. For these reasons, the investment democratization discussed in the GameStop story is notable because it follows a similar narrative in the cryptocurrency market that occurred just a short time prior.

Near the end of December 2020, market valuations in BTC-USD broke higher to reach marginal record highs just below $25,000. Less than three weeks later, those valuations skyrocketed by more than 72% (reaching highs just below $42,000 on January 8th, 2021) and many of these bullish rallies were driven by growing acceptance of cryptocurrency as a long-term store of value.

As a highly innovative form of digital currency, bitcoin is held electronically without the need for outside controls from external entities. Bitcoins are not printed in the way that fiat currencies can be printed, and this form of digital transaction has ushered in a new era in finance that has quite possibly given rise to one of most important investment revolutions in history. Perhaps the most important characteristic of the cryptocurrency space is the fact that its assets are decentralized, and this is one of the central differences when we compare bitcoin to the traditional fiat currencies. Since no government or institution controls the network, the protective democratization that characterizes bitcoin has put many individual investors at ease because the big banks will never hold control over the value of the assets.

For these reasons, it might not be a complete surprise that bitcoin came into existence in a period that followed the 2008 financial crisis. After Lehman Brothers unexpectedly filed for the largest bankruptcy in history, public confidence in large financial institutions was heavily damaged and government actions to bail-out some of the key players responsible for what ultimately became the credit crisis stoked high levels of mistrust amongst individual investors. At the time, the internet's most popular social media platforms still existed in forms that were relatively undeveloped, and this essentially meant that retail investors had a limited number of outlets through which to communicate and discuss new trading ideas.

Bitcoin's peer-to-peer infrastructure helped to solve many of these problems and the anonymous nature of its transactions helped to foster a sense of control that individual investors had never experienced in the past. Bitcoin investors can own multiple wallets (each with their own bitcoin address) without the need to register names, home addresses, or other types of information associated with personal identity. Ironically, that anonymity also comes with high levels of transparency because every bitcoin transaction is stored in the network (the massive general ledger known as the blockchain). Additionally, individual investors can capture these advantages with minimal trading fees because the idea of using a "middleman" has become largely obsolete. In the past, international transactions could be quite expensive. However, under the modern cryptocurrency framework, all transactions are borderless and the need to conduct monetary transactions through a series of linked banking entities might start to be viewed as an archaic concept that should be relegated to the dustbins of history.

For most cryptocurrency investors, these advantages have been apparent since bitcoin began trading in the open market. However, it has taken quite a bit of time for the institutional investment community to warm up to these ideas and to see real value in cryptocurrency assets. Famous examples include Warren

Buffett's characterization of bitcoin as "rat poison squared," which was accompanied with warnings for investors to avoid buying the cryptocurrency. Similar sentiments were expressed by Jamie Dimon (CEO of JPMorgan) when he said bitcoin is "a fraud" which creates investment risks that are "worse than tulip bulbs."

Here, it should also be noted that there really wasn't much room for misinterpretation in Mr. Dimon's comments because he doubled-down and clarified this negative viewpoint when he said this about that JPMorgan traders that might be considering long positions in bitcoin:

"I would fire them in a second, for two reasons: It is against our rules and they are stupid —and both are dangerous."

Perhaps not the most articulate (or persuasive) investment argument that has ever been made but the blanket dismissal of what could be one of the most significant modernizations in the history of the financial markets as "stupid" goes far beyond an inability to have a cogent debate on what, admittedly, might have been a controversial issue at the time. Specifically, this reluctance to accept the potential for digitization within the global currency markets might have initially discouraged investors from participating in some of the most tremendous asset rallies on record.

When Jamie Dimon made his misguided and ill-informed arguments that bitcoin could only be valuable for those with nefarious purposes, BTC-USD was trading at less than $4,500 and the rallies that followed just a short time later essentially confirm the inaccuracy of the institutional establishment's unwillingness to accept the potential advantages of digital currency assets. For those of us that might not remember Mr. Dimon's talking points, here is another gem for today's cryptocurrency investors to consider:

"If you were in Venezuela or Ecuador or North Korea or a bunch of parts like that, or if you were a drug dealer, a murderer, stuff like that, you are better off doing it in bitcoin than U.S. dollars... So, there may be a market for that, but it would be a limited market."

In clear contrast to these claims that cryptocurrencies can only exist within a "limited market," the total market cap of bitcoin broke above the $1 trillion in early 2021. As a comparative metric, we should understand that this valuation eclipsed the total market cap of JPMorgan, Citi, and Bank of America combined during the same period. To say that this comparative performance in the financial sector has worked as an appropriate measure of comeuppance for JPMorgan CEO Jaimie Dimon might be a significant understatement. Since 2018, it is true that bitcoin has experienced periods of weakness but the surging valuations in BTC-USD that we have seen recently make it abundantly clear that cryptocurrency volatility has been centered in the bullish direction.

By comparison, traditional assets (i.e. stocks in the financial sector) have failed miserably and this might help to give investors some sort of explanation for why JPMorgan announced the creation of its own cryptocurrency in 2019. Apparently, if you cannot beat them, join them —or just copy the retail trading community by creating a much less popular coin offering that fails to inspire global investors in any notable fashion. Ultimately, this reversal of fortune should provide cryptocurrency investors with at least some degree of confidence in the assertion that their investment strategies should never have been dismissed as "rat poison" that would be worse than "buying tulips in the 17th century."

But if a new asset's most severe critics wind up joining into the movement, cryptocurrency investors must have been doing something right —and it is obvious that these decisions have paid-off in ways that surpass the returns characterizing most of the assets that are currently available in the global financial market. Overall, prior attempts to suppress cryptocurrency investments through derision and dismissal have failed, and that the trading influence of the market establishment appears to be diminishing rather quickly. Bitcoin's historical price charts speak for themselves and it is difficult to make a convincing case for traditional stocks (especially those in the banking sector) when they consistently lose by such a wide margin.

Essentially, when investors are looking for reasons to explain why cryptocurrency skeptics have changed their tune on bitcoin and other digital assets, the answer appears to be glaringly uncomplicated: they simply had no other choice. At this stage, it's obvious that the reality of the situation has made both Jamie Dimon and the "Oracle of Omaha" look misguided due to the substantial potential for gains that was ignored for what can only be described as baseless reasons. However, these "expert" dismissals appear to have had little influence on willingness of the retail investment community to buy cryptocurrency. Ultimately, the broader bullish trajectory of BTC-USD in the months that preceded the GameStop short-squeeze shows that it will not necessarily be up to the traditional institutional investing establishment to determine whether the value of cryptocurrency assets will continue to produce substantial gains over time.

That said, there is a substantial amount of recent evidence which suggests that institutional investment in cryptocurrency is starting to build at an incredible rate. Even while these larger "establishment" players were clearly late to the game, a recent reversal of the bearish outlook amongst this group of investors might have set the stage for future short squeezes that take place in an entirely new sector of the market (the cryptocurrency space). However, those types of events are unlikely to occur near-term because the institutional investment community seems to have taken its cue from retail traders that were the market's earliest investors in crypto.

By the time Reddit's uprising against Wall Street hedge funds had become apparent in stocks like GameStop, market valuations in bitcoin had already seen rallies of as much as 300% during the prior three-month period. When viewed in combination with one another, all these trends suggest that dramatic trends were unfolding in several sectors of the market. These bullish price movements began while all three of the major U.S. stock benchmarks were trading near record highs. Perhaps it can be argued that the obvious disconnect between elevated price/earnings valuations on Wall Street weakened labor markets on Main Street left many retail traders in a position that called for decisive action. If these assertions are true, it can also be argued that the tremendous rallies that occurred in bitcoin worked as a precursor for the events that would occur in stock markets (i.e. shares of GameStop) just a few months later.

In all these ways, traders looking to analyze the long-term impact of the Reddit Rebellion must understand that these types of events rarely occur in isolation. If anything, the bullish wave toward social trading and the democratization of investments had been over a decade in the making. Clear clues for the social trading movements that would become the GameStop saga might have been signaled well in advance and primary evidence for this assertion comes from the fact that the retail trading community largely disregarded the "advice" of some of the most famous players in the Wall Street establishment (i.e. Jamie Dimon and Warren Buffett, among others).

Now that the political establishment has chosen its side (and called for investigations into the practices of brokerages like Robinhood), it seems as though there is little support for Wall Street hedge funds or the institutional investment community. If these trends continue, it also seems as though this weakened section of the market will be forced to capitulate in favor of the social trading community. In some ways, this could mean that we see a great deal more investment from hedge funds in bitcoin and other cryptocurrencies. However, the aftermath of the short squeeze initiated by the r/WallStreetBets community shows that the equities space will no longer be protected toward these trends toward democratization.

One event that could drastically alter this sanguine outlook might be seen if Congress starts to move toward tightening regulations in cryptocurrency markets. This possibility should be kept in mind for anyone that is interested in putting real money into any of these markets because the potential risk of loss is something that should never be forgotten by any trader (short-term or long-term). Thus far, we have seen little in terms of clear-cut rhetoric from government officials that appear to be focused on tightening regulations in cryptocurrency transactions. Of course, that does not mean that these types of events might not be seen in the future. But given the ways U.S. politicians (from both sides of the aisle) have voiced support for the retail trading community, we can see that an early precedent has been set and all this favors social trading and populist investment rather than hedge funds on Wall Street and the institutional investment community.

Ultimately, it is important for investors to understand the practical nature of cryptocurrency's place in both investment portfolios and in everyday consumer transactions. At its core, bitcoin (like many other cryptocurrencies) works through a network that is designed to operate as a functional digital currency that is fully decentralized. There is no authoritative administrator or central bank entity that is viewed as being in control of these operations because bitcoin's peer-to-peer network allows financial transactions to take place between users (while maintaining anonymity) without the use of an intermediary.

Bitcoin transactions work through a network of nodes that are secured through cryptography and allow important verification processes to take place. Ultimately, these transactions are recorded in a distributed ledger (a blockchain) that is publicly available and this helps users to protect themselves against the potential for hacking, fraud, and theft without the use of private cybersecurity systems. Bitcoins can be exchanged for products, services, fiat currencies or even other cryptocurrencies and they are created through a "mining" process (compiling bitcoin transaction records in the public ledger) that further rewards participants that enable this decentralized process to take place.

By the end of 2020, the number of active bitcoin users reached 432,000 "active entities," which is defined as a collection of wallets controlled by a one user that conducted a bitcoin transaction (sending or receiving) within a 24-hour period. Essentially, this figure tells us the number of people that are using bitcoin on a regular basis and this number has been rising steadily since the beginning of 2018. According to Matthew Dibb, founding member of Stack (a company that provides price trackers for cryptocurrency and cryptocurrency index funds):

"While the metric has breached highs not seen since 2017, it has done so gradually without 'bubble-like' growth. We take comfort in this when correlating address clusters with forward-looking price action."

Essentially, Matthew Dibb is suggesting that bitcoin prices tend to move higher when the number of regular users increases. Given the traditional supply and demand dynamics that define modern economic theory, this should not be surprising because widespread adoption of cryptocurrency tends to drive demand and this can be expected to lead to an increase in price valuations over time. According to Business Insider, roughly 106 million people around the world were using cryptocurrencies in January 2021 and a growing number of users in the Baby Boomer and Generation X demographics expressed an interest in using cryptocurrency.

A similar study from DeVere (a financial advisory company) found that nearly three-quarters of its clients over the age of 55 had invested in at least one cryptocurrency or were planning to do so in 2021. So, while the use of bitcoin and other cryptocurrencies is generally associated with younger investors (mainly those within the Millennial age demographic), recent data show that this is not really the case. As we can see, the reality is that cryptocurrency adoption has become increasingly prevalent amongst all age demographics and the consistency of this widespread increase in use will likely drive bitcoin prices higher over time.

Of course, bitcoin has also been criticized for its high potential for use in illegal transactions, erratic price volatility, and the significant amounts of electricity that is used by cryptocurrency miners. Many people in the financial analysis community have argued that bitcoin is in a speculative bubble that could hurt investors if there is a market crash in the future. Of course, these types of events remain a distinct possibility if we start to see government entities and central banks around the world that call for strict regulations on the use of cryptocurrency assets. However, the fact that these types of assets were able to grow in popularity in the first place just shows the growing need for fiat currency alternatives and this is why the recent implementation of cryptocurrency assets in the global markets has been a truly groundbreaking event.

Without much doubt, there are also several macroeconomic factors that have contributed to the rise of bitcoin and the popularity of decentralized trading activities. In the United States, government debt has been rising for decades and the country's debt-to-GDP ratio (which measures total debt in relation to annualized economic output) has been at (or above) 100% since 2013. In most cases, economists view this 100% threshold as a potential warning zone and when government debt levels rise above national output levels, it is often a signal that an oncoming financial crisis is quickly approaching. Ultimately, if global investors begin to lose confidence in the ability of the United States government to meet its debt obligations, financial analysts might start to argue that the U.S. dollar is on the verge of losing its status as the world's reserve currency. According to *Financial Times* columnist Rana Foroohar:

"The rise in popularity of highly volatile cryptocurrencies such as bitcoin could simply be seen as a speculative sign of this US Federal Reserve-enabled froth. But it might better be interpreted as an early signal of a new world order in which the US and the dollar will play a less important role."

In ways that are frighteningly similar to many other countries that are in decline around the world, the United States seems to show little interest in reversing the problematic trends associated with its mounting deficits. Moreover, global budgetary metrics appear to suggest that a large number of central banks will continue printing money at alarming rates even after the COVID-19 pandemic ends, although many of these quantitative easing programs are likely to be quite small when compared to the policy initiatives that have already been announced by the Federal Reserve.

As a result, these unsustainable macroeconomic trends seem to indicate that a long-term turning point is likely to be seen in fiat currencies (and in the value of the U.S. dollar, in particular). This is the type of environment that could help bitcoin gain in value if global investors continue to look for alternatives in digital currency markets. Many small businesses have already started to use cryptocurrency as a means to conduct international transactions and this has been particularly true in countries where it's difficult to secure U.S. dollars (i.e. Nigeria) or where excessive currency inflation has created instability within the broader economy (i.e. Argentina).

Bitcoin also appears to be making progress as a replacement for the U.S. dollar within consumer outlets as a primary medium of retail exchange. Recent news items show that Elon Musk's electric vehicle company Tesla, Inc. has made substantial bitcoin purchases and announced plans to accept bitcoin as a form of payment for its products. Of course, this follows announcements from PayPal and Venmo showing plans to accept cryptocurrency for all online payments and this suggests that a growing number of e-commerce transactions will be conducted using cryptocurrency as a medium of transaction. So while most today's bitcoin purchases are still made as an instrument for investment (rather than purchasing everyday items or paying bills), the overall trend in these areas seems to be changing.

Although some skeptics might argue that the recent surge in bitcoin valuations will eventually prove to be an unsustainable investment bubble, the rising popularity of cryptocurrency should send significant warning signals to central banks that are willing to print money at excessive rates. Of course, this is particularly true in the United States, and the Federal Reserve should not assume that the nation's reserve currency status is a given or that fiat currencies will be viewed as a favorable store of value in the future. Amongst both investors and consumers, cryptocurrency assets have been viewed with an increasingly elevated level of trust and it is likely that tech-savvy individuals will continue looking for an alternative to traditional fiat currencies until one is found (or simply invented).

All this recent evidence suggests that one thing is abundantly clear: cryptocurrencies have emerged a new class of assets that represents a formidable contender to the traditional store of value that is offered by the U.S. dollar. Largely ungoverned state authorities, we can see that the peer-to-peer networks associated with cryptocurrency assets have seen substantial growth in popularity as democratized, decentralized instruments for investment that incorporate practical applications for everyday use. Paradoxically, the COVID-19 pandemic only seems to have strengthened these views (at the global level) while making bitcoin sound less like "digital hype" and more like a viable alternative to fiat currencies that possess clear structural weaknesses.

Ultimately, the rise of bitcoin is both a symptom and reflection of long-term economic problems that have existed for many years — problems that have been papered-over by loose monetary policy (low interest rates) and artificially inflated asset prices high that developed through the accumulation of debt and the use of leverage in financial market investments. Unfortunately, these are the types of events that led to the 2008 financial crisis, hyper-inflation in the Weimar Republic, and many other economic catastrophes throughout history because, in the end, there are only three ways to control excessive debt loads: austerity, organic growth, or the printing of fiat currency via loose monetary policy.

If governments around the world continue printing fiat currency and fail to stabilize the broader trend in global markets, it seems likely that the recent rallies in bitcoin will continue to gain in momentum and cryptocurrencies (as an asset class) might gain better recognition as an alternative safe-haven store of value. Given this positive outlook for the long-term value of cryptocurrencies, it is important for investors to have a proper understanding of the various instruments that have started to show significant growth and popularity in financial markets. Cryptocurrencies often possess unique attributes that are quite different from one another and these important variations could play a significant role in the future of cryptocurrency investment and its effect on everyday retail transactions.

At this stage, most people are familiar with bitcoin, but they might be less familiar with the group of alternative coins (or altcoins) that are also included in the space. Ethereum is perhaps the most popular altcoin (based on market cap) and many of its principles (i.e. cryptography and distributed ledgers) share common traits with the operations of bitcoin. However, there are also key differences between these two networks. For instance, Ethereum transactions can include executable code, whereas the data associated with bitcoin transactions will generally be used for simple records and note-keeping.

Primarily, it should be noted that the algorithms that run each network transaction will be different for those using Ethereum. Bitcoin transactions run on the "SHA-256" algorithm while Ethereum transactions run using the "ethash" mining algorithm. Other key differences involve the amount of block time required for transactions on each network. When using bitcoin, transactions are confirmed in minutes whereas Ethereum transactions might only require a time period of seconds. For practical purposes, investors and consumers should also understand that these two networks operate with two broadly different goals in mind.

Specifically, bitcoin was designed to operate as a store-of-value alternative to fiat currency and to work as a medium of exchange in open markets. Ethereum's platform, on the other hand, was intended to transmit fixed contracts and immutable applications that can be facilitated by its own crypto payment system (using the ether cryptocurrency). Both Ethereum and bitcoin were designed to enable the use of digital currency. However, ether's functionality was not designed to establish a monetary system that worked as an independent alternative to global fiat currencies. Instead, ether was designed to monetize and facilitate the use of decentralized applications (dapp) and smart contracts that operate through the platform.

Essentially, Ethereum works as a use-case for a blockchain supporting the bitcoin network and therefore it should not necessarily be viewed as a BTC competitor. That said, ETH has held the second position (in terms of total market value) for most of its time freely trading in the open market, but its ecosystem is roughly one-fifth the size of bitcoin (as of March 2021, the total market cap for Ethereum was just over $200 billion).

In contrast to Ethereum, the XRP cryptocurrency is primarily known as a digital payment network. Specifically, XRP (designed by Ripple Labs) can be used in asset exchange, payment settlement, and as a remittance system (similar to SWIFT). These days many consumers are probably familiar with SWIFT as a method for conducting international money transfers that uses a network of financial intermediaries and banking entities to complete each transaction. Rather than implementing a blockchain mining system, the XRP network relies on its distributed consensus tools as they operate through the platform's server networks. Essentially, the Ripple platform conducts a poll and servers on the network determine the consensus outcome to validate each transaction.

The process makes it possible for XRP transactions to be confirmed in noticeably short periods of time without the need for additional verification that is conducted by a central authority. Overall, this allows XRP to maintain its status as a decentralized cryptocurrency while processing transactions at a rate of speed that is much faster than many competitors in the cryptocurrency space. Additionally, the Ripple platform generally requires much less power than the platforms used to conduct bitcoin transactions because there is no mining system for each coin. So while bitcoin transactions can take several minutes to reach the confirmation stage, market transactions using the XRP cryptocurrency can be validated in just a few seconds and with fees that are quite low when compared to the rest of its asset class.

In terms of market supply, there are 100 billion coins (all of which are pre-mined) and this is far greater than the total supply of bitcoin (at just 21 million). The fact that XRP coins are pre-mined also means that Ripple releases currency using mechanisms that are quite different when compared to the bitcoin mining system (which is essentially a proof-of-work mechanism). When miners find a bitcoin within the system, a new coin is added to the network. However, new releases of XRP coins are controlled through smart contracts that can be executed at any time. Initially, Ripple designed the system to release a maximum number of XRP coins each month (1 billion) and the current XRP circulation is seen above 50 billion coins. In any given month, any unused allotment of XRP coins is diverted into an escrow account. Essentially, this process prevents misuse and oversupply of the Ripple tokens, and it suggests that it will be quite a few years before the total supply of XRP will become available.

XRP is primarily used to transfer assets but many merchants are now accepting payments via the Ripple platform (similar to bitcoin). Each time a transaction is validated on the Ripple platform, a small charge (denominated in XRP) is deducted from the user's account. These users can either be a business or an individual but now appears that the use of the Ripple platform is most popular amongst banks. Of course, this might not be surprising, given the many similarities that exist when compared to the SWIFT payment systems for international transactions. For these reasons, XRP has seen tremendous growth from its use by financial institutions and the platform's easy-to-use payment system for cross-border transactions appears to be its key advantage when compared to other assets in the cryptocurrency space.

Litecoin is another popular cryptocurrency asset but the platform's size remains just a small fraction of what exists within the bitcoin ecosystem. As of March 2021, the total market cap of Litecoin amounts to roughly $13.5 billion (which is less than 1.5% of the total bitcoin market cap during the same period). Litecoin even pales in comparison to the total market cap of Ethereum but it should be remembered that it took a few years for bitcoin to cross the $10 billion threshold. Essentially, this shows that Litecoin assets have achieved a level of value that is quite respectable and has shown significant growth over the last few years.

Apart from its size, the Litecoin payment system also shows significant differences in the ways it is distributed through the market. Interestingly, the Litecoin platform can accommodate a maximum of 84 million coins (which is four-times the number of bitcoins that will eventually exist in the system). However, it is not entirely clear how this will impact the coin's value in the future because each Litecoin is infinitely divisible (similar to bitcoin). Essentially, this means that Litecoin users will be able to use the cryptocurrency to make small payments and asset transactions, so there is a high level of functional utility that can be associated with the coin.

At its inception, the Litecoin payment system was designed with speedy transactions in mind and when we make comparisons to the bitcoin payment system, it seems that these goals have been achieved. Specifically, the average transaction confirmation period for activities conducted through the Litecoin platform amounts to less than three minutes. This is essentially the amount of time that is required for each block to be verified and added to the public ledger. In contrast, the same transaction confirmation period on the bitcoin platform amounts to nearly nine minutes. Litecoin's efforts to prioritize transaction speed might work to its benefit in the future as it could make it easier for everyday purchases to be conducted by merchants using this system.

However, the most significant differences between bitcoin and Litecoin can be found in the cryptographic algorithms used by each system. Specifically, Litecoin transactions are conducted using Scrypt (which is a relatively new algorithm) while bitcoin transactions rely on the much more widely known SHA-256 algorithm. In practical terms, the most important difference between these two systems lies in the ways each system mints a new coin. Litecoin is like bitcoin in that miners are required to process and confirm transactions before they can be added to the blockchain. However, these processes can require incredible amounts of computing power and this can often become a barrier for some users that might not have suitable computing resources to conduct these procedures in an efficient manner.

In general, the SHA-256 algorithm is considered more complex than Scrypt and it allows for a broader parallel processing in each transaction. Those mining for bitcoin typically use Application-Specific Integrated Circuits (or ASICs) to mine BTC in an efficient manner. Unlike the simple GPUs and CPUs that worked as predecessors, ASICs are systems that can be designed specifically for the process of mining bitcoin. Unfortunately, the complexity of these processes has made it much more difficult for everyday users to mine bitcoin (unless they join mining pools).

In contrast, Scrypt was created as a way of allowing users to avoid the customized hardware tools that are typically associated with mining based on ASICs. Ultimately, this could mean that Litecoin has provided a system that is much more accessible for everyday users that are interested in mining the cryptocurrency. Although some Scrypt ASICs have already been made available in the market, a high percentage of the mining processes used within the Litecoin system are conducted using GPUs or CPUs and this adds to Litecoin's reputation as being more easily accessible to many users.

Since its inception, one of the most common criticisms levied against the bitcoin platform has been its slow processing speed for individual transactions. Overall, these limitations have created significant rifts between bitcoin miners and developers because these slow processing speeds could have a negative impact on the cryptocurrency's market valuation and ability to scale in the future. In 2017, mining pools responsible for 80-90% of bitcoin's computing power conducted a vote and decided to incorporate segregated witness technology (or Segwit3) as a way of reducing the amount of data that requires verification in each block. Essentially, this fix removed signature data associated with each transaction and attached it to an extended block.

Since this information accounts for as much as 65% of the data in every block, these changes represent a substantial improvement in the cryptocurrency market's ability to overcome the speed limitations traditionally associated with bitcoin transactions. Within the bitcoin community, discussions calling for an increase in block sizes continued and, by February 2019, bitcoin's average block size grew to 1.3 MB. However, these figures started to decline by the following year and a general lack of sustainable progress forced members of the bitcoin community to seek alternatives that would allow for better scalability for the cryptocurrency in the future.

Ultimately, these issues led to the development of bitcoin cash, but many miners and developers had reservations about SegWit3x (and its follow-up technology, SegWit2x). Specifically, these concerns were based on bitcoin's inability to achieve true scalability and maintain the roadmap that was originally designed by pseudonymous bitcoin creator Satoshi Nakamoto. Eventually, bitcoin developers called for a "hard fork" and this led to the creation of bitcoin cash (BCH) as a new cryptocurrency. Bitcoin cash operates through its own blockchain and includes a critical distinction in its ability to implement larger block sizes.

Originally, bitcoin cash was able to speed up the transaction verification process using block sizes of 8 MB and this included adjustability features to ensure the viability of each chain. In 2018, bitcoin cash experienced a 4x increase in its maximum block size (to 32 MB) but the actual block sizes on the network have remained relatively small when compared to the new upper limit. Because of these advancements, bitcoin cash is capable of processing transactions at a rate that is much faster than its parent predecessor and this has helped to reduce fees for the transactions that are made on the network.

When compared to bitcoin, the network that handles transactions in bitcoin cash is able to process many more operations each second. However, the larger block sizes that are associated with bitcoin cash also open the system to certain vulnerabilities that might not be present when conducting transactions using bitcoin. Additionally, the total market cap of bitcoin cash (at less than $10 billion, as of March 2021) is well below that of bitcoin, and this means bitcoin cash is associated with much lower liquidity levels that could impact usability in real-market situations going forward.

As the debate on the topics of transaction processing speeds, block sizes, and future scalability continues, new innovations have defined the space. Near the end of 2018, bitcoin cash had its own hard fork, and this led to the creation of bitcoin SV as another derivation of the bitcoin universe. Essentially, bitcoin SV was designed to maintain Satoshi Nakamoto's original vision for bitcoin (according to what was outlined in the original whitepaper) while, at the same time, allowing for important modifications that can facilitate better transaction speeds and potential scalability in the future. Clearly, developers will continue to make modifications that allow for advancements that promote the everyday usability of digital currencies and these are the types of changes that are likely to define the cryptocurrency landscape in the years ahead.

However, that does not mean that cryptocurrency is without risk or that certain barriers to widespread adoption will not be seen in the future. Clearly, the use of cryptocurrency in consumer markets has become a topic of contentious debate amongst economic policymakers around the world. Many governments have maintained a favorable stance that has been friendly toward investors and consumers participating in the cryptocurrency market. But others have shown reluctance toward openly accepting these assets as potential investments while refusing to issue guidance on the proper use of cryptocurrency in consumer markets.

In some countries (i.e. Russia, Colombia, and China) cryptocurrencies have been banned in both investment and consumer markets. Critics have argued that these moves to block the use of cryptocurrency have resulted from fears that government entities in these regions would lose power and economic authority to a decentralized majority. In the United States, government entities have adopted an outlook on cryptocurrencies that has been mostly favorable.

However, not many formal rules have been officially introduced and most of the regulatory debate that has taken place within individual agencies. In other words, these discussions on the viability (and legality) of cryptocurrencies has included bodies like the Federal Trade Commission (FTC), the Financial Crimes Enforcement Network (FinCEN), the Internal Revenue Service (IRS), the Securities and Exchange Commission (SEC), and the Department of Treasury. But since these agencies have little communication with one another, there has not been much agreement in terms of how cryptocurrencies should be regulated.

For example, FinCEN does not consider bitcoin (or any other cryptocurrency) to be legal tender. However, FinCEN does consider cryptocurrency exchanges as vehicles for monetary transfers (which means that crypto exchanges would fall under its jurisdiction). As another example, the IRS has established policies which characterize cryptocurrencies as personal property (which makes cryptocurrency assets subject to taxation). Despite these measures, the federal government in the United States has not exercised pre-emptive constitutional powers that regulate assets transmitted via blockchain platforms. Instead, the federal government has left these questions of legality up to state governments (as is often the case with financial regulations).

Ultimately, this lack of clarity has left the door open to the possibility of new regulation at a later date. But, in some cases, these measures have already started. In mid-2015, New York became the first example of a state government willing to enact regulations for companies using virtual currencies. By 2019, more than 30 states had introduced some form of legislation surrounding the sale or purchase of bitcoin or other currencies using blockchain distributed ledger technology. But while only a few of these states have passed these measures into law, several more states have created task forces to further study blockchain technology and its potential use in both investment and consumer markets.

For both investors and consumers, this potential for surprise regulation in the future creates an added element of uncertainty that can make it difficult to start buying cryptocurrencies in large amounts. In terms of the long-term impact these uncertainties can have on market prices, it is clear that demand constraints can negatively affect valuations, prevent assets like bitcoin from reaching higher levels, and reduce the viability of cryptocurrency in consumer markets. Moreover, it is entirely possible that the prospect of tighter regulation in the United States could inspire a wave of similar activities in other countries that look to the American legal system as a model for its own legislation.

However, any further efforts to outlaw bitcoin (or tax cryptocurrencies at excessive rates) might have unintended consequences and accelerate the populist rebellion that has started to thrive within various social media communities. Essentially, it would not be surprising if governments taking these sorts of actions were accused of acting in anti-democratic ways and protecting their own authority with efforts to stop the global trend toward investment decentralization.

In this case, whose interest would it appear that the government has in mind —theirs or the people's? What would be the public's response to such government action (both in the United States and around the world)? Would these decisions simply favor the classically authoritative big-government agenda, or could systemic efforts to regulate cryptocurrency initiate the final push for undecided fence-walkers to finally admit to the practical superiority of fiscal conservatism?

Of course, these are all important questions to consider for anyone with plans to buy cryptocurrencies or to make future investment decisions in equity markets using next-wave social media platforms. Since we are still relatively early in the course of these trends, the easy answer is that the jury is still out —and it might be too early to imagine exactly how new regulatory proposals will impact the decisions of both retail consumers and market traders. However, at this stage, it seems undeniable that these are the central issues that we will all be forced to contemplate going forward.

Ultimately, the surprising emergence of cryptocurrencies and meme stocks seems to have worked as a simple reflection of the continuous push-pull that has always existed between the traditional establishment (i.e. Wall Street or big-government entities) and the common majority (i.e. retail traders and social media platforms that continue to grow in terms of both power and popularity). No matter which side of the argument you find yourself navigating, one thing should be clear at this stage: the next major financial market inflection point has officially arrived —and the next few years will be critically important in defining the way the investment world will look in the future.

CHAPTER 8

5 Reasons It Should Matter to You

Reason 1: *Financial success has been made practically attainable for all people in our society.*

During the early days of the Brexit campaign, citizens of the United Kingdom adopted a rallying cry that was voiced by protesters within the movement: "Take back control." For many, this sentiment expressed a feeling that the needs of a silent majority had been ignored and largely forgotten by their representatives in government. Of course, in any properly functioning democracy, each citizen is supposed to have control over his or her own fate and this requires the ability to vote for laws that work in each person's best interests. In many ways, the Brexit campaign represented a new opportunity to take back control from disconnected, far-off political entities that could not be held accountable for inefficiencies in the democratic process.

By the end of 2020, many of those same sentiments seemed to be building to a boiling point within the global financial markets. Over the last few years, social trading platforms have slowly gained prominence in terms of both market influence and real-world impact by allowing everyday investors to "take control" of their financial future. In large part, these trends have rendered traditional financial institutions obsolete and reduced the market-moving dominance that has been enjoyed by hedge funds for as long as anybody can remember.

In today's modern trading world, investors do not need to operate through the Wall Street establishment to gain access to relevant market information or well-credentialed investment advisors. Instead, social media platforms have opened the door for discussions about high-level investment strategies and analysis of real-time market data that can be used to develop a viable approach to navigate price trends in global markets. These days, all it takes is a smartphone and an internet connection to gain access to all the educational materials that might be required to start investing and regain control of your financial future.

Within this modern environment, trading apps such as Robinhood have surged in popularity because of their ability to reduce costs and offer access to sections of the trading community that have been overlooked in the past. At the same time, Robinhood's unpopular response to the unanticipated market activity that took place during the Reddit Rebellion shows just how quickly the tide can turn when the champion of a disenfranchised majority reverses course to serve the best interests of Wall Street's institutional establishment. However, the historic Reddit Rebellion has unveiled many key questions (and uncovered many critical weaknesses) with respect to what has traditionally been recognized as the status quo in the world of investment.

In the past, the ability to successfully invest in the financial markets seemed to be reserved for gurus with privileged access to real-time financial information capable of impacting asset prices. Most people understand that global markets are fast-moving and that the "smart money" is often able to capitalize on newly emerging economic events the moment they occur. Unfortunately, this is often to the detriment of those in the retail trading community because market trends tend to reach a point of maturity by the time these investors are typically able to execute a position in open markets.

All of this explains why pension funds and wealthy individuals were usually among the most significant stockholders guiding price trends in the pre-digital market environment. However, this systemic exclusivity amongst the Wall Street elite has been eroded by improved access to social communities full of like-minded investors and an increase in the democratization of app-based trading tools. As a primary example of these emerging trends, the r/WallStreetBets trading forum (and its two million active users) managed to ignite an astounding rally in GameStop share prices that cost bearish hedge funds roughly $20 billion less than one month and worked in direct opposition to the stated goals of the institutional investing establishment.

At the time, GameStop was not widely considered to be a well-positioned company capable of sustainable earnings growth and most analysts on Wall Street thought that the stock was unlikely to achieve an elevated market valuation relative to its key industry competitors. GME share prices languished near $5 for several years leading up to the historic short-squeeze event in 2021 and it seemed that very few in the market believed that the brick-and-mortar dinosaur would be able to re-invent its business model in ways that could keep the company competitive within its industry.

However, it also appears that the "democratization of investment" has fully disrupted the influence of various institutional entities and has created an increased potential for unprecedented occurrences within various aspects of the financial world. For these reasons, the events that have defined the GameStop saga will probably not mark the final chapters of this story. What began as a group of disjointed internet personalities discussing companies and conducting their own due diligence on a stock quickly turned into a fascinating cultural phenomenon that moves the market in ways analysts haven seen in many years (if ever).

A combination of retail investing, gaming culture, viral memes, social media platforms, and a desire to hit Wall Street where it hurts quickly launched into a revolutionary movement that, quite possibly has changed the investment landscape forever. As a company, GameStop rallied from small-cap status into the large-cap stratosphere in a matter of weeks and the move literally turned many retail traders into unexpected millionaire investors overnight. Of course, all of this occurred as large portions of the Wall Street establishment was forced to endure significant losses and one hedge fund lost over 50% of its assets (roughly $8 billion) in just one month.

In the aftermath of these historic events, everyone seems to be asking themselves many of the same questions: Was the GameStop saga a temporary flash in the pan that will eventually result in Wall Street's hedge funds reclaiming their collective throne and dominating the efforts of smaller traders? Or did these events usher in a new era of investment with trends in stock markets influenced by trading groups from social media platforms (rather than the traditional fundamental earnings metrics)? Given the extent of the media coverage this story has already witnessed in the discussion of these topics, it looks as though the genie is out of the bottle and that the traditional market dynamics have been redefined for many years to come.

Reason 2: *Traditional stock valuation models have been broken and financial market trends have finally been liberated by the masses.*

In its earliest incarnations, the Robinhood trading platform operated under a slogan that emphasized the democratic nature of its trading base: "Investing for Everyone." Of course, this implies that it is no longer up to the institutional minority to determine appropriate valuations for assets trading on stock exchanges.

Amongst the analyst community on Wall Street, GameStop was considered to be in "serious trouble" even before COVID-19 pandemic lockdowns forced the company to close its doors to the public. According to Business Insider technology writer Ben Gilbert:

"The world's biggest video game retailer, GameStop, is in serious trouble. In the past 12 months, the company's stock value has dropped by two-thirds — from about $15 in January 2019 to under $5 by January 2020 — and it reshuffled its C-suite.

Like Blockbuster Video and Tower Records before it, GameStop faces major challenges to its business model from the internet. As more people buy video games through digital storefronts, fewer buy games on physical discs from GameStop."

Moreover, these types of negative criticisms continued even after GameStop was seen trying to enact remedies that were designed to modernize its operations. Investment research from bearish analysts on Wall Street continued to argue in favor of the short side of the GME trade even in cases where the company's underlying fundamentals were showing improvements. In these ways, the institutional establishment was able to shape the narrative to the benefit of active short positions that were open in the market.

Of course, these heavily biased reports worked to the clear disadvantage of both shareholders and a struggling retail company trying to change its business during a period of pandemic-driven uncertainties. But that did not stop the trading community at r/WallStreetBets from conducting its own analysis and establishing positions on the other side of the trade. As former White House communications director and bitcoin financier Anthony Scaramucci described the situation in a tweet:

"We are witnessing the French Revolution of Finance."

Once the walls started caving-in (and large hedge funds started losing billions of dollars), institutional entities on Wall Street began to adjust their own operations in ways that suggested the financial analysis of the retail trading community finally deserved to be acknowledged as important. Specifically, trading algorithms were developed by data providers to monitor market investment flows driven by various social media platforms so that hedge funds would be aware of any changes in momentum (in real-time). According to a recent article from the Financial Times:

"Hedge funds accustomed to poring through arcane corners of

earnings reports in search of companies to bet against are turning their sights on foul-mouthed online message boards in an effort to stay ahead of day traders who have started beating them at their own game."

One of these entities mining data from various social media platforms is Quiver Quantitative, which is a provider that uses language processing algorithms to gauge the market relevance of trending topics in internet communities like r/WallStreetBets. When asked about the growing interest Wall Street has expressed in scraping data from Reddit's investment communities Quiver Quantitative CEO James Kardatzke explained:

"Everyone is looking at Melvin [Capital] and these other hedge funds that went short as a cautionary tale. You need to be aware of where retail might be able to blow up a position, or where there might be a real surge on retail interest."

In the past, it would have been quite rare to monitor the investment flows from entities outside of the Wall Street establishment. But, as is often the case, losing a significant amount of money can provide valuable lessons and black-box trading entities can be used as a line of defense to gain a sense of where sentiment within the broader investing community might be travelling next.

Longer term, there is mounting speculation which suggests that future legislation might prevent hedge funds from executing short strategies at levels that exceed 100% of the total outstanding shares for a company. Of course, this could help to curb some of the potential volatility that now exists in financial markets, but we will also see Wall Street's hedge funds closely monitor social media platforms to identify potential short squeezes before they occur.

Clearly, popular trading communities like the r/WallStreetBets forums have become a risk management issue for hedge funds and therefore they have risen to the top of the agenda for those within the institutional establishment. As a result, it appears likely that these entities will be forced to devote more resources to the goal of understanding where majority sentiment amongst retail investors is heading in the future. When asked about the role of social media platforms in financial markets, David Lebovitz, JPMorgan global market strategist recently explained:

"Now you will be able to tap into less traditional sources of information to figure out how retail is positioned. This is a segment of the market that has been historically opaque, and now we're beginning to flash a light around."

At this stage, it has become abundantly obvious that the thoughts and intentions of all traders (even those with the smallest account sizes) can carry weight while influencing the dominant trends in market prices. Additionally, regulatory bodies at the highest levels of government have taken notice and released quite fervent commentaries criticizing the current state of the market. As Congresswoman Maxine Waters, Democrat from California and Chairwoman of the House Committee on Financial Services, explained:

"We must deal with the hedge funds whose unethical conduct directly led to the recent market volatility and we must examine the market in general and how it has been manipulated by hedge funds and their financial partners to benefit themselves while others pay the price."

To calm the potential for stock market volatility, further actions to design legislation that works to the advantage of the investing majority seems more and more likely in the years ahead. All of this suggests that traditional models for valuation in equity markets could change dramatically in the future. Previously, common valuation methods like an assessment of price-to-earnings metrics or discounted cash flow models might have controlled the narrative for stocks at any given time.

Of course, these investment strategies tend to focus on fundamental factors like revenues, profits, assets, and liabilities, so any outlook suggested by these factors could often drive trends in stock prices on both short-term and long-term time horizons. But while this might continue to be the case in many instances, the democratization of markets has really opened the door for the use of alternative strategies that rely more heavily on "majority rule," rather than the market outlook that might be published by a Wall Street investment bank.

In other words, stock valuation models based on traditional metrics might begin to carry less weight in guiding real trends in market prices. Given the disruptive outcome of the GameStop story, stock prices might be dictated to the changes in sentiment expressed by investors using social media platforms and this type of activity could have substantial ramifications on every aspect of asset valuation practices in the future.

Reason 3: *The GameStop saga reveals new cultural opportunities for reuniting a deeply polarized nation.*

Following one of the most contentious presidential elections in the history of the United States, many political commentators were surprised by the ways the GameStop story managed to unite prominent members of the country's major parties. Both Democrats and Republicans were able to "get behind the cause" as lawmakers criticized the restrictive actions of Robinhood in preventing retail traders from buying certain stocks.

Spectacular rallies in GameStop were fueled by irregular trends in options trading and a reactive surge in bullishness that gained momentum so quickly that platforms like Robinhood and Interactive Brokers felt the need to act by halting orders on the long side of the market. However, accusations of unfair trading practices rattled policymakers in Washington and members from both parties threatened to act to ensure that similar circumstances do not occur again in the future.

These instances of bipartisanship have encouraged many people that have hoped for reconciliation following a period of deep political turmoil in the United States. At the highest levels, White House Press Secretary Jen Psaki signaled a willingness to work with Congress in an effort to reduce the potential for disruptive volatility in stock markets, telling reporters:

"There is an important set of policy issues that have been raised as a result of market volatility in [GameStop], and we think congressional attention to these issues is appropriate and would welcome working with Congress."

This high level of interest at the upper levels of government has been encouraged by a widespread consensus in the House of Representatives and the Senate. This surprising consensus has been voiced by opposing members of both bodies that rarely agree on contentious issues. According to Ro Khanna, Democratic Representative from California:

"This entire episode has demonstrated the power of technology to democratize access to American financial institutions, ultimately giving far more people a say in our economic structures. This also showed how the cards are stacked against the little guy in favor of billionaire Wall Street Traders.

Instead of investing in future technologies to help America win the 21st Century, Wall Street poured billions into shorting this stock to crush this company and put workers out of business. The future of this country lies in that access and equality across every sector of our economy."

Similar sentiments have been expressed by Donald Trump Jr., and people with high-level positions in government have favored the concerns of retail traders over those expressed by Wall Street hedge funds. In some ways, this is ironic because it was the hedge fund establishment that lost most of the money during the heightened stock market volatility associated with GameStop shares:

"It took less than a day for big tech, big government and the corporate media to spring into action and begin colluding to protect their hedge fund buddies on Wall Street. This is what a rigged system looks like, folks!"

To get a sense of the incredible unity these events have inspired, we can compare the comments of Donald Trump Jr. to those expressed by Senator Sherrod Brown, Democrat from Ohio, and Chairman of the Senate Banking Committee. Following announcements that the Senate would begin to hold hearings on the "current state of the stock market," Senator Brown said:

"People on Wall Street only care about the rules when they're the ones getting hurt," Brown said in a statement. "American workers have known for years the Wall Street system is broken – they've been paying the price. It's time for the SEC and Congress to make the economy work for everyone —not just Wall Street."

Fortunately, the need for a closer examination into the inner workings of Wall Street extended beyond the groups of politicians tasked with the operations of the banking industry. In a letter to the SEC, Elizabeth Warren (Democratic Senator from Massachusetts) said:

"I am deeply concerned that these casino-like swings in the value of GameStop and other company shares are yet another example of the gamesmanship that interferes with the 'fair, orderly, and efficient' function of the market, raising obvious questions about public confidence in the market and those trading in it."

So, while the Chairman of the Federal Reserve (Jerome Powell) largely refused to take an aggressive stance and release public comments about issues related to the GameStop story, many prominent politicians were quite willing to make their voices heard and side with one another to protect smaller traders from the traditional dominance of large players on Wall Street. Essentially, this is a meeting of the minds that has been quite unusual in recent years and therefore our ability to unite behind a common cause could be strengthened by the GameStop story over the long-term.

Reason 4: *Widespread backlash against the restrictive actions of Robinhood shows that retail traders will not be bullied by Wall Street in the future.*

In response to all these public comments from prominent politicians in both big-ticket parties, Robinhood has chosen not to push-back in defense of its prior actions to restrict trading activities amongst retail investors. When asked for public comment, Robinhood instead directed financial reporters to a blog post written to quell the issue. The post was given the title "Keeping Customers Informed Through Market Volatility" and it outlined some of the concerns expressed by both the political establishment and the retail trading community, in saying:

"Our mission at Robinhood is to democratize finance for all. We're proud to have created a platform that has helped everyday people, from all backgrounds, shape their financial futures and invest for the long term."

For many critics, this response failed to directly address the concerns experienced by retail investors during the GameStop short squeeze. However, the fact that these responses could not be perceived as controversial in any way shows that the retail trading community has gained the upper hand and that Robinhood lacks sufficient explanation for its prior actions. Of course, all of this begs an answer to one critical question: Has the power dynamic fully shifted in favor of the market's smaller private investors? Perhaps not entirely.

However, recent cultural events suggest that a major sea-change is taking place which will allow retail investors to have a much greater influence with respect to price trends in stock markets. For anyone that is currently active in these markets, the long-term impact of these events should not be underestimated. In fact, many institutional names on Wall Street have started to allocate budgeting resources to monitor newly emerging trends on various social media platforms. These plans are being executed to identify potential market-movers in stock markets while trading opportunities still exist.

For many, this outcome probably is not much of a surprise, given the amount of media coverage the GameStop story has generated. Of course, this includes Elon Musk's now-famous one-word tweet "GameStonk!!!" which helped shares of GME double in value even before the following trading session had even started. These bullish price movements clearly favored the retail trading community using the r/WallStreetBets social media forum and worked to the detriment of the institutional hedge funds that were caught on the wrong side of the trade.

Now that retail traders have become aware of the true power they can yield within the open market, it seems reasonable to expect that this previously disenfranchised community will no longer be bullied by the Wall Street establishment in any sustainable way. That said, it is also important for the retail trading community to remember that this is no time to rest on their laurels and assume that every trade will wind up in favorable territory. If the situation with Robinhood has taught us anything, it is that there will always be unforeseen obstacles in the market, and these can have a negative impact on any trades that are currently open in the market.

For these reasons, it is a good idea for retail investors to have trading accounts open with more than one brokerage. When Robinhood restricted buying activity in shares of GME stock, it would have been possible for retail traders to increase bullish exposure using other brokerages that had not implemented the same restrictions. Remember, these are essentially private companies that can enact new policy decisions based on their own interests and discretion. As a result, having our investment "eggs" in multiple "baskets" can give traders greater power when certain types of trading restrictions are implemented.

Essentially, these are the types of practical strategies that traders should take away from the entire GameStop saga. Whether or not a person had exposure to the stock, it is always important for smaller investors to protect themselves from the potential for market manipulation. Based on what we have seen in Robinhood's response to the unprecedented price volatility in GameStop, it should be clear that many of the restriction problems retail traders encountered could have been avoided by using more than one trading broker.

Of course, some of these issues might not be so concerning for buy-and-hold investors that are able to move in and out of positions over long-term time horizons. However, there are times when even these investors might need to make quick decisions to effectively manage their investments and the potential for position restriction can certainly create problems for traders that are working on shorter-term time horizons. While this approach might not be guaranteed to guard against the effect of market manipulation in all circumstances, the ability to spread financial assets over several different trading accounts can help retail traders to mitigate the impact of enhanced price volatility in many different market situations.

In cases where it makes sense to enter several positions at once (or to make quick exits from those positions), having access to multiple brokers makes it less likely that retail traders will fall victim to artificially imposed outages like those imposed by Robinhood during the GameStop surge. Essentially, this is just another way that retail traders can take back control from the institutional establishment and this is another reason which explains why the GameStop story has provided lessons that can offer a lasting impact for everyone in the global investment community. Overall, the lasting impact of these events can be confirmed by the fact that prominent leaders in government have come together with bi-partisan agreements that are aimed at providing retail traders with better control over their investments. In the end, the widespread backlash that has been initiated against the restrictive actions of Robinhood shows that it will not be so easy for Wall Street to bully the retail trading community in the future.

Reason 5: *The Reddit Rebellion reveals new opportunities for individual traders to invest in cryptocurrencies and profit from a decentralized future.*

For centuries, the ability of individuals to effectively manage their investments has been stunted because control over the global monetary system has been dictated by what essentially amounts to a monopolistic system run by national governments. On a smaller scale, the dominating impact of Wall Street hedge funds and institutional investors has been able to artificially influence trends in stock markets so that profits can accumulate on one side of the trade. These historical tendencies have mostly favored the establishment and worked to the detriment of smaller investors.

However, the recent actions of the r/WallStreetBets trading community have upended many of these traditional expectations and set the stage for a new world order that could revise the market's investment authoritative expectations for many years to come. In all these ways, Reddit's Rebellion against the actions of the Wall Street establishment has set the stage for a long-term reversal in the power dynamic that has existed between individual investors and the much larger corporate or governmental authorities that have always had a stranglehold on the overriding trends seen in global asset valuations.

Ultimately, these long-term trend reversals might be so significant that they extend far beyond the realm of small-cap stocks in U.S. equity markets. Given the proximity of the GameStop story in relation to the meteoric rise in bitcoin valuations near the end of a pandemic-influenced trading year in 2020, it is easy to see why many financial analysts have described this as a confluence of events as a scenario that could inspire investors to flock toward decentralized assets and favor the safe-haven protection of cryptocurrencies. Clearly, the long-lasting relationship that has existed between individual monetary investments and the reach of big government is showing cracks in its foundation.

For these reasons, the steady erosion of market control has reduced the monetary authority of large corporate entities and governmental institutions. However, this historical monopoly over the monetary system no longer needs to maintain its control over the lives of everyday citizens. Bitcoin (and other cryptocurrencies) can provide a viable alternative for peer-to-peer exchange that is both autonomous and fully decentralized. But if recent events like GameStop, the Reddit Rebellion, and the ceiling-shattering rally in crypto might seem like a temporary change in markets - just remember that there is really nothing that is novel or unique about digital currencies.

Ultimately, these assets have a lot in common with credit cards or consumer transactions conducted through digital payment systems like PayPal, Stripe, Payoneer, Skrill, and countless others. Of course, these types of payment instruments have been around for decades and they have proven themselves to be viable systems capable of protecting consumers against fraud while streamlining the transaction process for everyday buying and selling activities. But what might be truly novel is the fact that the masses are now in control of the technology that is guiding the market. According to David Nadig, CIO of ETF Trends:

"The herd has learnt how to use the technology of Wall Street against them. Retail investors have access to technology, market information and margin to a degree that was not seen two decades ago during the dotcom day-trading boom. Wall Street is being challenged by retail."

Bitcoin just seems to be the next step in the evolution of digital payment systems and the fact that the digital currency's recent surge was followed by the historic GameStop short squeeze shows that what is under attack now is the institutional establishment and its longstanding control over the everyday lives of consumers. These events simply mark the culmination of a classic David vs. Goliath story that has become visible in multiple asset classes and has stretched to all corners of the world. As Congressman Jeff Duncan (Republican from South Carolina) has explained:

"The wealthy and well-connected get cover at the expense of everyday Americans making individual decisions in the market. This is Wall Street collusion at its worst. We are witnessing a modern-day David vs. Goliath story. All the American people want is fairness – from the little guy all the way up to large corporations. They want to know the system isn't rigged against them, and that rich Wall Street types play by the same set of rules as the rest of us."

Of course, these sentiments help to explain why there is something that is truly revolutionary in bitcoin's decentralized, peer-to-peer system of exchange. In a truly short period of time, cryptocurrency has evolved from a small-scale movement driven by computer scientists, cryptographers, and "cyber-punks" into a phenomenon that has become more and more mainstream. Essentially, the ethos that underlies the development of cryptocurrency assets can offer us a blueprint for change that has the potential to completely redesign the entire financial system and, in fact, change the nature of the internet itself.

As technology continues to evolve and change, the move from centralized services to decentralized operations might at first seem unfamiliar or untrustworthy for many people. But it is important to remember that many things might seem to be permanent fixtures in the market until an innovative disruption comes along and makes us realize how inefficiencies might have defined our prior actions. Since its inception in the 1960s, the internet has experienced many fundamental changes, and this shows that the status quo can be changed at any time.

More than ever before, smart, and talented individuals are working together to drive innovation on the internet and the growing acceptance of bitcoin amongst investors and consumers has turned the march toward decentralization into a goal that is more attainable than ever before. If these trends continue, the market's center of gravity will increasingly focus on the empowerment of each person that lives within the global economic system. In these ways, we can see that cryptocurrencies have the potential to divert control from the hands of the few and grant new powers to the destiny that defines the fate of the many.

In the next decade, the blueprint laid by the bitcoin blockchain has been revolutionary in terms of its ability to redefine the ethos of the internet while fostering choice, opportunity, and independence amongst the previously disenfranchised investors. For now, this well-publicized decentralization of the financial market has become a phenomenon that has been nothing short of awe-inspiring for most of the people involved. Overall, this process has created many new millionaire investors within the retail trading community and caused rising levels of anxiety amongst some of the most famous money managers operating hedge funds on Wall Street.

Where these trends go from here might be anybody's guess. Traditionally, governments tend to find a way to reign-in market exuberance and the institutional establishment tends to find a way of emerging victorious through long-term profitability strategies. But now it seems that a majority of the most prominent political figures in the U.S. government have developed a vested interest in enacting new regulation that protects the needs of retail investors, so we will more than likely start to see hedge funds proceed with caution in terms of their willingness to establish large short positions on stocks trading in the small-cap category.

In the end, the prevailing themes for investors following the r/WallStreetBets saga revolve around historic paradigm shifts that have worked in opposition to the elite minority of the past and in favor of majority control over modern financial markets that is truly collective in nature.

As the important lessons from the Reddit Rebellion story show, these shifts toward economic modernization have been powerful enough to push-back against the long-term market dominance that has been enjoyed by the institutional investing establishment for as long as any of us can remember in practical terms.

In this case, hedge fund analysts on Wall Street that were predicting a sharp decline in value for GameStop stock were really hit where it hurts when their assessments were proven to be wrong in quite a dramatic fashion. Ultimately, these incorrect assessments cost the institutional establishment billions of dollars and proved that a dynamic power-shift has finally taken place in the global financial markets. Just as political democracies often face turmoil that redefines the modern approach and changes the outlook going forward, this process of democratization within the global investment community has opened the door for new investment classes and an alternative approach to valuing asset prices in the open market.

As things currently stand, the cryptocurrency asset class looks likely to experience much greater recognition for its technological advantages during the aftermath of the GameStop short squeeze. What we are witnessing now is a widespread democratization of assets in the global financial markets that cannot be dismissed as a simplistic or transitory one-off event. As outdated shibboleths continue to fall victim to the influential disruptions of blockchain technology, our traditional notions of authority and financial power that have been controlled by the Wall Street establishment will need to be redefined in the years ahead. Almost certainly, these changes will work to the advantage of cryptocurrency investors that entered these markets at the ground-level because it is now clear that the Reddit Rebellion has revealed new opportunities for individual traders that are ready to invest in a more decentralized future.

REFERENCES

Collins, T. (2021). *gamestop-and-the-dangerous-game-of-gamma-squeezes*. From Realmoney.thestreet.com: https://realmoney.thestreet.com/investing/stocks/gamestop-and-the-dangerous-game-of-gamma-squeezes-15546125

Dictionary.com. (n.d.). *https://www.dictionary.com/e/memes/stonks/#:~:text=In%20internet%20slang%2C%20stonks%20is,to%20comment%20on%20financial%20losses*. From www.dictionary.com: https://www.dictionary.com/e/memes/stonks/#:~:text=In%20internet%20slang%2C%20stonks%20is,to%20comment%20on%20financial%20losses

Hayes, A. (2021). From Investopedia: https://www.investopedia.com/terms/s/shortselling.asp

Leech, O. (n.d.). *https://www.coindesk.com/wallstreetbets-reddit-group*. From www.coindesk.com: https://www.coindesk.com/wallstreetbets-reddit-group

Pachter, M. (n.d.). *https://www.businessinsider.com/gamestop-failing-store-tour-shows-flawed-business-2019-8#theres-some-good-news-for-gamestop-the-next-generation-of-game-consoles-is-coming-in-2020-and-that-means-gamestop-will-likely-last-for-at-least-another-several-years-*. From Wedbush: https://www.businessinsider.com/gamestop-failing-store-tour-shows-flawed-business-2019-8#theres-some-good-news-for-gamestop-the-next-generation-of-game-consoles-is-coming-in-2020-and-that-means-gamestop-will-likely-last-for-at-least-another-several-years-

Russolillo, S. (2016, December 3). Irrational Exuberance: Alan Greenspan's Call, 20 Years Later. *The Wall Street Journal*. From https://www.wsj.com: https://www.wsj.com/ar-

Shiller, R. J. (2......nal Exuberance.

Thompson, D. (2021). The Whole Messy, Ridiculous GameStop Saga in One Sentence. *The Atlantic*. From https://www.theatlantic.com/ideas/archive/2021/01/why-everybody-obsessed-gamestop/617857/

White, C. M. (n.d.). From U.S. Securities and Exchange Commission: https://www.sec.gov/news/speech/mjw-speech-032114-protecting-retail-investor

---

[1] Market Capitalization is calculated by multiplying the total number of a company's outstanding shares by the current stock price.

Printed in Great Britain
by Amazon